....101 WAYS TO....

stitch | craft
create
FOR ALL OCCASIONS

BIRTHDAYS ♥ **WEDDINGS** ♥ **CHRISTMAS**
EASTER ♥ **HALLOWEEN & MANY MORE...**

D&C
David and Charles

www.stitchcraftcreate.co.uk

CONTENTS

INTRODUCTION

This collection of 101 craft projects provides endless inspiration for all the most important celebrations in life and throughout the calendar year. Try your hand at a wide range of crafts, including knitting, papercraft, crochet, applique, sewing, embroidery, cake decorating, beading, patchwork and quilting.

Helpful time and difficulty indicators accompany each project so you can choose the designs most suited to your skill level or to the time you have available to craft.

Many of the projects take an hour or less, some take minutes, and all can be completed easily in a weekend. Please note that times given for making projects do not include drying times:

up to 2 hours

3-4 hours

over half a day

All of the projects are ideal for those just getting started, although some are even more beginner friendly than others:

no special skills required

assumes you know the basics but still very simple to make

these may stretch you but they are well worth that extra effort

Cross stitch charts are included at the back of the book. All templates for the projects featured in this book are available at: **www.stitchcraftcreate.co.uk**.

Use these projects as a springboard to your own creativity as so many of the designs are easy to adapt to any occasion. Mix and match colours and motifs to create something truly unique for your celebration.

BIRTHDAY

PARTY HAT CUPCAKES
by Ruth Clemens

These lovely cupcakes make a great alternative to a big birthday cake – each is decorated with a homemade party hat and streamers cake topper.

You Will Need

Six cupcakes

White sugarpaste

White sugar florist paste (SFP)

Green, blue and purple gel paste colours

Buttercream

Fluted circle cutter 5.5cm (2¼in) diameter

Round cutter 5mm (³⁄₁₆in) diameter

Large open star piping nozzle

Disposable piping bag

1. Knead together equal amounts of white sugarpaste and white SFP. Colour portions light green, blue and purple, leaving the remainder white. Roll out the light green paste to 2mm (³⁄₃₂in) thick. Cut out six fluted circles and set aside to dry.

2. Shape six cone-shaped hats 3cm (1⅛in) high by rolling white paste first into a ball, tapering the top and then flattening the base. Secure each hat onto the green discs using a little water.

3. Create the details for each hat in blue, purple and green. Roll a 7mm (⁹⁄₃₂in) ball for the top and secure with a dab of water. Roll a thin sausage 7cm (2¾in) long and wind around the base. Roll out a little paste to 1mm (¹⁄₁₆in) thick, cut out five dots and add around the side of the hat.

4. Roll out a little blue and purple paste very thinly. Use a roller cutter to cut strips 10cm (4in) long by 5mm (³⁄₁₆in) wide. Wind gently around a cocktail stick then slide off.

5. Add a purple and blue streamer to the side of the party hat. Fit the open star nozzle to a piping bag and fill with buttercream. Pipe swirls to the tops of each cupcake and place your cupcake toppers in position.

1 HOUR

EASY PEASY

VINTAGE-STYLE BADGES
by Jennifer Grace

These name badges provide an elegant way for guests to get to know each other at any birthday gathering. They would also make great place cards for the party table.

You Will Need

Patterned paper

Scraps of vintage-style floral fabrics

White card

Brown ink pad

Small letter stamps

Cream sewing thread

Large safety pins

1 HOUR

GET STUCK IN

1. Make a 7.5cm (3in) diameter circle template and use to draw enough circles, one for each guest, onto the back of the patterned paper. Cut out the circles and ink the edges of each with the brown ink (choose a nice rich brown).

2. Using a 6cm (2⅜in) diameter circle template draw the same number of circles onto the back of the floral fabric. Cut out.

3. Machine stitch the fabric circles onto the middle of the paper circles using the cream thread and stitching in a spiral from the edge to the centre.

4. For the name tags, cut small strips of card approximately 3cm x 1.5cm (1⅛in x ⅝in). Use small letter stamps and the brown ink to stamp the names of your guests onto the card strips.

5. Ink the card edges with the brown ink. Use tacky craft glue to stick the name tags to the centre of the fabric circles. Leave until the glue has dried.

6. To finish, use tacky craft glue to stick a large safety pin to the back of each badge. Leave to dry.

SLICE OF FABRIC CAKE

by Ellen Kharade

This fabric cake is a lasting reminder of the birthday celebration and can be used long after the event as a useful pincushion. There are two sweet designs to choose from.

You Will Need

White felt

Patterned fabric

Pink felt flowers

Pink ribbon, ric rac and small pompoms

Green and pink pearl and seed beads

Piece of foam 5cm (2in) deep

2 HOURS

GET STUCK IN

1. Use the template to make patterns for the cake top, side, base and back. Place the cake top pattern on top of the foam, aligning one edge with the edge of the foam; draw around the shape and use a craft knife to cut along the marked lines.

2. Using the patterns, cut a cake top from patterned fabric, and cut two sides, one base and one back from white felt.

3. With right sides facing, pin the long side of the patterned fabric to the long side of one of the felt side pieces. Machine stitch in place. Now pin the other long side of the patterned fabric to the long side of the second felt side piece, and again machine stitch in place. Pin the felt back piece to the short side of the patterned fabric and machine stitch as before. Pin the side seams together, and once again machine stitch in place to complete the cover.

4. Pull the cover over the foam. Place the felt base beneath the foam; pin the seams and hand stitch. To hide the join, hand sew ric rac across the fabric change.

5. To decorate the cake slice, hand sew a length of ribbon around the edge making sure that it is centred; and embellish the top with pearl and seed beads, felt flowers and small pompoms cut in half.

Full-size templates for this project are available at: www.stitchcraftcreate.co.uk

BIRTHDAY

LADYBIRD CUSHION
by Ellen Kharade

Any child would be delighted to receive this cute creature as a birthday gift, but it also makes a fun and quirky decoration for a party.

You Will Need

Red and brown patterned fabrics

Black fabric

Black felt and black yarn

Fusible interfacing

Red and brown ric rac

Toy filling

Red stranded cotton (floss)

3 HOURS

GET STUCK IN

1. Use the templates to make paper patterns for the ladybird's wings, small body, main body, head, and body spots (two large spots and two small).

2. Use the paper patterns to cut two wings (one reversed) from the red patterned fabric, one small body from the brown patterned fabric, one head and one main body (back) from the black fabric.

3. To make the body front, pin the wings to the small body and machine stitch, then pin and machine stitch the head in place.

4. Iron interfacing onto the back of the black felt. Pin the spot patterns to the felt, cut out, then fix onto the wings by ironing. Machine stitch around the edge of the spots then decorate the with blanket stitch worked with red embroidery thread.

5. Pin and machine stitch ric rac across the head and body. Pin the body front to the main body (back) with right sides facing. Machine stitch around the edges leaving a 13cm (5in) gap for turning. Turn the ladybird through the right way, press and stuff with toy filling until nicely rounded. Sew up the gap with ladder stitches.

6. Make two pompoms from black yarn and attach to the head.

Full-size templates for this project are available at: www.stitchcraftcreate.co.uk

BIRTHDAY

CHILDREN'S PARTY BAG
by Chloe Adcock

These embellished party bags are perfect for filling with sweets to delight younger guests. You could even add the children's names to personalize each bag.

You Will Need

Co-ordinating patterned papers

White expandable envelopes size A4 (US letter)

Silk ribbons in assorted colours

Balloon punch

30 MINUTES

GET STUCK IN

1. Trim off the glue flap from an envelope. Fold both sides in and the base up by approximately 3cm (1⅛in), using a bone folder to score the lines for a crisp edge.

2. Open the envelope and with your hand inside push out the scored lines to form two flat sides. Repeat for the score lines at the bottom of the envelope to form a flat base; fold in the bottom corners and stick to the base.

3. You now have a rectangular bag. Score and fold over the open top edge. Punch two holes for the ribbon to thread through once the bags have been filled.

4. Cut a piece of patterned paper the same width as your bag and approximately 6cm (2⅜in) high and use double-sided tape to stick it to the bag front. Punch out balloon shapes from co-ordinating paper and adhere to the decorative band.

5. Cut thin strips of paper and curl around a pencil to create the streamers. If desired, cut out paper letters to spell the name of the recipient and use a glue pen to attach to the front of the bag.

6. Repeat steps 1–5 to make as many bags as you have guests at the party. Fill the finished bags with toys, sweets and small gifts, and tie a ribbon through the pre-punched holes to seal.

BIRTHDAY

BUTTERFLY CARD

by Jane Millard

This monochrome birthday card is decorated with a stitched panel and stamped 3D butterflies. Try changing the colours of the card to suit the season.

You Will Need

Patterned and plain black card

White and light coloured patterned papers

Cream single-fold card 13.5cm x 13.5cm (5¼in x 5¼in)

Butterfly stamps

Black ink pad

Decorative edge punch

1. Cut a piece of patterned black card measuring 13cm x 13cm (5in x 5in) and attach to the front of the single-fold card.

2. Cut a piece of plain black card measuring 13cm x 10cm (5in x 4in), and punch along the long edges using the decorative edge punch. Position the punched card in the centre of the front of the card blank using a little double-sided tape to secure it.

3. Cut a wide strip of white patterned paper and machine stitch on top of the punched card strip, making sure that it is centred.

4. Stamp three butterflies onto light coloured patterned paper and carefully cut out. Use small adhesive foam pads to stick the butterfly bodies onto the stitched panel making sure they are evenly spaced. Then lift and shape the wings of the butterflies.

30 MINUTES

GET STUCK IN

BIRTHDAY

BIRTHDAY BUNTING
by Emily Rodger

Hand-sewn bunting provides a great centrepiece for a birthday celebration, especially when decorated with pretty felt appliqué shapes.

You Will Need

75cm (30in) pink printed cotton fabric 110cm (45in) wide

2.5m (2¾yd) of fuchsia pink 2.5cm (1in) bias binding

Pink felt

Pink stranded cotton (floss)

2 DAYS

FANCY A CHALLENGE

1. Cut out 26 triangles from the pink printed cotton fabric measuring 18cm (7in) along the bottom and 20cm (8in) through the centre.

2. Use the appliqué templates to cut a few decorative shapes from pink felt. Pin the motifs onto the right side of half of the triangles so that the top of the appliqué shapes are approximately 3.5cm (1⅜in) from the top edge of the triangles.

3. Sew the motifs in place using decorative stitches, such as running stitch or blanket stitch, with two strands of pink embroidery thread.

4. Take an appliquéd triangle and place on top of an undecorated triangle, with right sides facing and the raw edges aligned. Machine stitch along the angled sides only, then turn through to the right side. Repeat to make 12 more pennants.

5. Fold the bias binding in half so that it is half its original width. Pin the open tops of the triangles in the fold of the binding, starting about 18cm (7in) in from one end and placing the pennants next to each other.

6. Sew all the way along the folded binding making sure that all of the open pennant tops are sewn in. Hang up the finished bunting.

Full-size templates for this project are available at: www.stitchcraftcreate.co.uk

MACRAMÉ BRACELET
by Dorothy Wood

This elegant macramé bracelet, made using half hitch knots and large glass beads for decoration, would make a stylish 18th birthday gift.

You Will Need

Large-hole light blue glass bead

Six 6mm antique silver round metallic beads

Blue cotton cord

2 HOURS

FANCY A CHALLENGE

1. Cut two lengths of cotton cord each measuring 30cm (12in), and one length measuring 150cm (60in). Take the two short lengths and tape at each end onto the work surface positioning them side by side. These are your 'core' cords.

2. Tie the longer length of cord around the two core cords using an overhand knot and taking care to make sure that the tails are the same length. Pass the left tail under the core cords and pull through leaving a largish loop on the left side of the core cords. Pass that tail over the tail on the right side.

3. Lift the right tail over the core cords and down through the loop on the left side. Pull the cords through to make a half hitch knot. Work several more knots to make a 1cm (⅜in) block of macramé.

4. Thread a silver bead onto the core threads. Take the tails either side of the bead and work another 2cm (¾in) block of macramé. Repeat twice.

5. Slide the large-hole glass bead onto the twisted cord. *Add a silver bead and work another 2cm (¾in) macramé block. Repeat from *.

6. Work 1cm (⅜in) of macramé to finish. Trim tails to 2cm (¾in). Remove the tape and form the bracelet into a round shape with the tails facing in opposite directions.

7. Tie a 30cm (12in) length of cord around the four core cords. Work a 2cm (¾in) length of macramé. Add drops of strong glue to secure the tails making sure the slider still slides. Tie the core threads together at each end. Trim tails once dry.

DECORATIVE GIFT TAGS

by Jenny Arnott

There is no better way to present your birthday gifts than with a beautiful handmade gift tag crafted from decorative papers and ribbons.

You Will Need

Co-ordinating patterned papers

Cream card size A4 (US letter)

Scraps of floral fabrics

Ric rac, narrow ribbon and button embellishments

30 MINUTES

EASY PEASY

1. Cut identical tag shapes measuring 6cm x 12cm (2⅜in x 4¾in) from a selection of co-ordinating patterned papers.

2. Use small pieces of floral fabric, ribbons, ric rac and buttons to decorate each tag. Stitch or glue the embellishments directly onto the paper tag shapes.

3. Sew around the outside edge of each tag shape using straight machine stitch with a co-ordinating colour thread.

4. Mount the paper tags onto cream card using double-sided tape and trim the edges. Punch a hole in the top of each tag and thread with a co-ordinating ribbon.

Full-size templates for this project are available at: www.stitchcraftcreate.co.uk

BIRTHDAY

NUMBER BADGES
by Claire Garland

A hand-knitted button cover embellished with a felted number makes a colourful badge to be proudly worn by the birthday boy or girl.

You Will Need

Set 3.5mm (US size 4) double-pointed needles

Small amount of Rowan Creative Focus Worsted in your chosen colour

Flat button 2.5cm (1in) diameter

Large safety pin

Scraps of brightly coloured felt

1. Knit the button cover following the pattern below:

Cast on 6sts onto one needle then complete the cast on as follows:
Step 1: Hold needle with sts in LH.
Step 2: Hold 2 empty dpns parallel in RH.
Step 3: Slip 1st cast on st purlwise onto the dpn closest to you and off the needle in the LH, then slip the next cast on st onto the dpn furthest away and off the RH needle. Repeat step 3 until all 6sts are divided onto the 2 parallel dpns, 3sts on the front dpn and 3sts on the back
Slide sts to the other ends of the dpns, working yarn at back.
RS facing, cont working in the rnd,
beg by knitting the sts on the back dpn – work sts over 2 dpns, using a 3rd dpn to knit with:
Rnd 1: (inc) Kf&b, k1, kf&b, kf&b, k1, kf&b. 10sts (5sts on each needle). Place marker.
Rnds 2, 4, 6, 7: K.
Rnd 3: (inc) Kf&b, k3, kf&b, kf&b, k3, kf&b. 14sts
Rnd 5: (inc) Kf&b, k5, kf&b, kf&b, k5, kf&b. 18sts
Rnd 8: (dec) Sl1, kl, psso, k5, k2tog, sl1, kl, psso, k5, k2tog. 14sts
Rnd 9: K14.
Rnd 10: (dec) Sl1, kl, psso, k3, k2tog, sl1, kl, psso, k3, k2tog. 10sts
Ease button into the knitted cover.
Rnd 11: K10.
Rnd 12: (dec) Sl1, kl, psso, k1, k2tog, sl1, kl, psso, k1, k2tog. 6sts

2. Cut the yarn leaving a 10cm (4in) tail. Close the opening using the grafting technique.

3. Felt the badge: soak with hot water, rub in hand soap, rinse out soap, squeeze out water, and rub until yarn is matted together to give you the felted look you are after – if the badge is still very damp, rub it in between a tea towel. Keep checking the badge for shape as you rub, re-moulding it to make the edges perfectly round. Re-shape the badge one last time before placing it on a radiator to dry.

4. Once the badge has completely dried, sew the safety pin to its reverse. Now add a felt number to the front. Using the number templates as a guide, copy your chosen number onto a piece of felt and cut out. Sew in place by working horizontal stitches around the edge of the number.

1 HOUR

GET STUCK IN

Full-size templates for this project are available at: www.stitchcraftcreate.co.uk

PRETTY PINK PIG

by Ali Burdon

Give this simple hand-stitched felt pig as a present for a child's birthday – its cute ears and curly backstitch tail will appeal to all ages.

You Will Need

Pink felt

Scraps of white felt

Pink, brown and white stranded cotton (floss): DMC colours 309, 433 and blanc

Toy filling

2 HOURS

GET STUCK IN

1. Use the template to make a pentagon template from card, and use to cut out 14 pentagons from pink felt. Also cut four 1.5cm (⅝in) diameter circles and four strips measuring 15cm x 1cm (6in x ⅜in).

2. Use three strands of thread for all stitching. To make the nose tack (baste) the circles together and pin in the centre of a pentagon. Blanket stitch around the edge of the circle stack to secure them in place. Use brown thread to make two French knots for the nostrils.

3. To make the legs, roll up each of the four felt strips tightly, oversewing at the join and around the bottom edge.

4. To make the ears, take two pentagons, sew lines of running stitch along one edge and gather up.

5. To make the pig's body, join 11 of the pentagons together, oversewing the edges for a ball with one pentagon missing. Turn right side out and stuff with toy filling.

6. Sew the nose section in place, keeping the seam on the outside to create a ridge. Add a little more filling before finally closing.

7. Cut two small white felt circles for the eyes, using white thread to stitch in place and embroidering the pupils with brown thread. Sew on the ears and the legs, making sure that these are very secure, then backstitch a curly tail to finish.

Full-size templates for this project are available at: www.stitchcraftcreate.co.uk

BIRTHDAY

BALLOON MINI CAKE
by Ruth Clemens

Mini cakes make a great party favour and you can celebrate in style with a burst of bright balloons for decoration.

You Will Need

One 6.5cm (2½in) mini cake

Buttercream

10cm (4in) diameter cake card

White sugarpaste

White sugar florist paste (SFP)

Red, green and blue gel paste colours

White royal icing

Disposable piping bag

No. 2 piping nozzle

24-gauge florists' wire

Cake pick

Medium and small rose petal cutters

Bright blue ribbon

1 HOUR

GET STUCK IN

1. Prepare your mini cake for covering by applying a thin layer of buttercream. Roll out the white sugarpaste to 5mm (³⁄₁₆in) thick on a surface lightly dusted with icing sugar. Use the paste to cover the mini cake smoothing to a fine finish with a cake smoother.

2. Position the covered cake in the centre of the cake card and secure with a dot of buttercream. Trim the base of the cake with bright blue ribbon secured at the back with a pearl-headed pin.

3. Knead together equal amounts of white sugarpaste and SFP. Colour one third red, one third blue and one third green. Roll out one colour at a time to 2mm (³⁄₃₂in) thick. Using the medium rose petal cutter, cut out one of each colour for the large balloons. Using the small petal cutter, cut out four of each colour for the small balloons. Using a sharp knife cut out small triangles in each colour to match the body of the balloons. Set aside to dry.

4. When the balloon pieces have dried out, begin the assembly. Cut six pieces of florists' wire approximately 15cm (6in) long. Fit a piping bag with a no. 2 piping nozzle and fill with white royal icing. Secure one piece of wire along the back of one medium balloon and one small balloon in each colour using the royal icing. Allow the icing to dry.

5. Once the icing has fully dried, turn over each balloon and secure the small triangle in place for the balloon tail, again using a bulb of royal icing. Add a small reflection mark to the front of each balloon. Leave to allow the icing to dry fully.

6. Secure the remaining balloons in a random colour pattern around the side of the cake using royal icing. Pipe white ribbon tails and a small reflection mark for each.

7. Insert the cake pick into the centre of the top of the cake. Gather together the wired balloons and arrange in a spray. Secure the ends of the wires together by using the a piece of wire to wind around them, and insert into the cake pick.

8. Roll two short thin sausages of red and blue paste and position around the top of the cake pick, securing in place with a light brush of water.

STAR GARLAND
by Anna Wilson

Make the birthday boy or girl the star of the party with this garland of five fabric stars, stuffed with polyester filling, decorated with buttons, and suspended from ribbon.

You Will Need

Red patterned fabric

White and red fabrics for appliqué

White fusible interfacing

Five buttons

Printed ribbons

Wide red satin ribbon

Polyester filling

3 HOURS

GET STUCK IN

1. Using the large star template, cut 10 stars from the red patterned fabric.

2. Iron the fusible interfacing to the back of the white and red appliqué fabrics. Cut five medium stars from the red fabric and five small stars from the white fabric. Take one of the large stars and appliqué on a medium star, then appliqué a small star on top.

3. Sew a button to the centre of the star appliqué. Repeat to make four more appliquéd stars.

4. Cut five 10cm (4in) lengths of printed ribbon. Fold a ribbon length in half and place the raw edges at the top of one of the appliquéd stars (loop pointing inwards). Place an undecorated star on top, right sides facing, and pin together. Repeat for the remaining stars.

5. Sew around the edges of the joined stars, sewing straight across the ribbon and leaving a small opening on one side for turning through to the right side. Stuff the stars with polyester filling before sewing the gaps closed.

6. Thread the stuffed stars onto the wide red satin ribbon. Pin the stars an equal distance apart and sew in place.

Full-size templates for this project are available at: www.stitchcraftcreate.co.uk

BIRTHDAY

PENNY FARTHING CARD
by Charlotte Addison

This vintage design makes an ideal birthday card for male friends or relatives – it's a little work of art with its metal embellishments.

You Will Need

Cream single-fold card size C6

Scrap fabric

Vintage-style papers and butterfly stickers

Black embroidery thread

Long fasteners

Sprocket gear embellishments

2 HOURS

GET STUCK IN

1. Using the template cut out the hill from vintage-style papers and stick to the card blank front.

2. From scrap fabric, cut out a large circle to make the bigger wheel for the penny farthing. In pencil, draw the outline for the penny farthing's handles and for its frame. Using backstitch, embroider over the outline with the black embroidery thread.

3. Using a sprocket for the bicycle's smaller wheel, secure with a long fastener. Position your circle of scrap fabric, and secure with a sprocket in its centre using a long fastener to hold it in place. Stitch around the edge of the fabric wheel to keep it flat.

4. Embellish your card with butterfly stickers, or you could draw on some clouds freehand.

Full-size templates for this project are available at: www.stitchcraftcreate.co.uk

BIRTHDAY

VALENTINE'S DAY
&
ANNIVERSARY

3D PAPER HEARTS

by Sue Trevor

A set of pretty dimensional heart decorations, made in three different sizes, will make quite an impact at any romantic celebration.

You Will Need

24 sheets of double-sided patterned paper 30.5cm (12in) square

Pink sewing thread

Pink cotton cord

30 6mm silver jump rings

15 glass beads

1 HOUR

GET STUCK IN

1. Make card templates of the three different heart shapes required. For each decoration three same-sized paper hearts are used. From a pack of 24 sheets of paper you will be able to make 19 decorations.

2. Use the large heart template to cut large hearts from nine sheets of paper. Cut eight sheets of patterned paper in half and use for cutting out 15 long, thin hearts.

3. Divide the remaining sheets of paper into quarters, and use to cut 30 small hearts. Place the cut out hearts together in matching groups of three. Machine stitch a line down the centre of each group of hearts.

4. Make a hole at the top and bottom of each heart using a large needle. Attach a jump ring through each hole. Tie and double knot a 12cm (4¾in) length of cotton cord to each jump ring.

5. Make a loop for hanging at the top cord. Thread a glass bead onto the bottom cord and tie with a double knot to secure. Your heart decorations are now ready to hang.

Full-size templates for this project are available at: www.stitchcraftcreate.co.uk

VALENTINE'S DAY & ANNIVERSARY

BIRDS CENTREPIECE

by Marion Elliot

Decorate the table for an anniversary party with this lovely centrepiece. Group two pairs of birds together as shown, or use them separately for corner tables or shelves.

You Will Need

Two sheets white card size A4 (US letter)

Patterned papers

1 HOUR

GET STUCK IN

1. Make a tracing of the birds template. Fold a sheet of card in half. Place the tracing along the folded edge and redraw over the traced lines to transfer the birds to the card.

2. Cut out, using a craft knife for the fiddly interior area. Score the card down the centre, then fold in half. Repeat for the second piece of card to give you two pairs of birds.

3. Use the wing, chest, eye, leg and beak templates to cut eight of each from the patterned papers. Glue the patterned paper details in place to either side of each bird using the photograph as a guide.

4. Place the folded edges of the bird pairs together to make the centrepiece. You can apply a little PVA glue along the folded edges if you wish to keep them in place.

Full-size templates for this project are available at: www.stitchcraftcreate.co.uk

VALENTINE'S DAY & ANNIVERSARY

FLOWER BASKET CAKE
by Ruth Clemens

Try changing the ribbon and flower colours of this mini cake to suit any anniversary. Remember to leave the sugarpaste embellishments to fully dry before assembling.

You Will Need

One 6.5cm (2½in) mini cake

Buttercream

7.5cm (3in) square cake card

White sugarpaste

White sugar florist paste (SFP)

Red, green and brown gel paste colours

White royal icing

Disposable piping bag

Circle cutter 5cm (2in) diameter

Red ribbon

1½ HOURS

GET STUCK IN

1. Apply a thin buttercream layer to the cake. Roll out the white sugarpaste to 5mm (³⁄₁₆in) thick and cover the cake smoothing to a fine finish. Use a dot of buttercream to secure the cake to the centre of the cake card; trim with red ribbon.

2. Knead together equal amounts or white sugarpaste and SFP; divide into four equal parts. Leave one quarter white; colour the others red, green and brown. Roll out brown paste to 2mm (³⁄₃₂in) thick, cut a circle, and place over a rolling pin to make a basket shape.

3. For leaves, pinch small green paste balls into teardrop shapes. Gently flatten and score a line down the centre. Make 12, each 1cm (³⁄₈in) long. For flowers, roll red and white thin paste sausages 2cm (¾in) long. Flatten one long edge and roll up from the end. Trim excess at base. Make four red and six white. Cut a brown paste basket handle measuring 6mm x 6cm (¼in x 2³⁄₈in); secure to the inside of the basket. Line the edge with leaves and fill with flowers attached with a little piped royal icing. Make tiny leaves to fill in between. Attach the basket to the mini cake with a little royal icing.

ROMANTIC RUFFLED CARD
by Jennifer Grace

This flirtatious card is ideal for any romantic occasion. It's quick and easy to make, and all you need is some coloured crepe paper and glue!

You Will Need

White single-fold card size C6

Red, white and pink crepe paper

Permanent glue runner

30 MINUTES

EASY PEASY

1. Cut two strips of pink and red crepe paper and one strip of white, each measuring 10.5cm x 3cm (4¼in x 1⅛in) with the grain running vertically along the strips.

2. Run the permanent glue runner across the bottom of the card 3cm (1⅛in) from the base and stick on the first strip of red crepe paper.

3. Stick each strip of crepe paper approximately 3cm (1⅛in) above the last, working your way up to the top of the card.

4. Adhere the crepe paper strips in the following order: pink, white, red, pink. Stick the crepe strips along their top edge only leaving the bottom edge unstuck for frills.

5. Once all the strips have been glued in place gently stretch the bottom edges by pulling them horizontally between your fingertips, a little at a time, to give you the ruffled effect.

VALENTINE'S DAY & ANNIVERSARY

SWEETHEART APRON
by Denise Mutton

This retro-style reversible apron has a large heart-shaped pocket on one side. It's perfect for keeping your clothes clean when cooking up a romantic dinner for two.

You Will Need

Fabric A: 0.5m (20in) 112cm (45in) wide

Fabric B: 1m (40in) 112cm (45in) wide

Red sewing thread

Fusible interfacing

2 HOURS

FANCY A CHALLENGE

1. To make a template for the reversible apron panels, cut a piece of paper 67cm x 40cm (26in x 16in) and use a large dinner plate to round off one of the bottom corners of the longest edge. Fold the paper in half and mark the second corner to match. Use this pattern to cut the apron panels from fabrics A and B.

2. Cut four pieces of fabric B measuring 9cm (3½in) long to the width of the fabric. For a frill, sew two fabric B strips to form one long strip; and press.

3. Fold the frill strip lengthwise (wrong sides facing); press. Repeat for the two remaining strips to make the waistband/ties.

4. Lay one apron panel right side up; attach frill, raw edges matching, pinning tucks at 2.5cm (1in) intervals; tack (baste) in place. Cut two fabric B hearts; interface one. With hearts right sides together, sew around edge leaving a small gap for turning, then slip stitch closed. Attach heart to centre of fabric A, leaving top open to form a pocket.

5. Place the apron panels together right sides facing, so that the frill stays between the panels. Pin and sew; turn right side out. Sew gathering stitches along the top edge. Match middle of waistband to middle of gathered edge. Measure 5cm (2in) beyond the frill edge at either side and mark with a pin. From end of ties sew raw edges to the pinned marks. Turn the ties right way out and press. Sew waistband to gathered edge of apron (right sides facing). Turn over and slip stitch the other side of the waistband in place. Press to finish.

Full-size templates for this project are available at: www.stitchcraftcreate.co.uk

VALENTINE'S DAY & ANNIVERSARY

LITTLE HUGGING HEART

by Claire Garland

This cute knitted and felted heart is the perfect size to pop into the pocket of a loved one to show them how much you care.

You Will Need

Four 3.5m (US size 4) double-pointed needles

1 x 50g ball Wash + Filz It Fine red

Toy filling

Two buttons

Black sewing thread

2 HOURS

GET STUCK IN

1. Knit the hugging heart following the pattern below:

Arm
*Cast on 8sts onto one needle.
Step 1: Hold needle with sts in left hand.
Step 2: Hold 2 empty dpns parallel in right hand.
Step 3: Slip 1st cast on st purlwise onto the dpn closest to you and off the needle in the left hand, then slip the next cast on st onto the dpn furthest away and off the RH needle. **
Repeat step 3 until all 8 sts are divided onto the 2 parallel dpns, 4sts on the front dpn and 4sts on the back.
Slide sts to the other ends of the dpns, working yarn at back.
RS facing, cont working in the rnd,

beginning by knitting the sts on the back dpn – work sts over 2 dpns, using a 3rd dpn to knit with:
Rnd 1: K8. Place marker.
Rep last rnd 14 times. Cast off. ***
Knit the other arm as before from * to ***.

Heart

Cast on 4 sts. Cast on as Arm from * to **.
Repeat step 3 until all 4 sts are divided onto the 2 parallel dpns. Slide sts to other end of dpns. Work in the round.
Rnd 1: (inc) Beg with the 2sts at the back, kf&b 4 times. 8sts
Rnd 2: K8.
Rnd 3: (inc) Kf&b, k2, kf&b, kf&b, k2, kf&b. 12sts
Rnds 4, 6, 8, 10, 12: K.
Rnds 5, 7, 9, 11: Increase 4sts on each rnd; increasing 1st at beg and at end on each dpn. 28sts
Rnds 13, 14: K.
Rnd 15: K7, slip next 14sts off needles and onto a length of spare yarn, knit next 7sts.
Rnd 16: (dec) *Sl1, kl, psso, k3, k2tog, sl1, kl, psso, k3, k2tog. 10sts
Rnd 17: K10.
Rnd 18: (dec) Sl1, kl, psso, k1, k2tog, sl1, kl, psso, k1, k2tog. 6sts**
Cut yarn leaving a 10cm (4in) length. Join using the grafting technique.

Very lightly stuff the heart with the toy filling.
Divide 14sts from other side of heart equally over 2 needles, rejoin yarn, k14 then knit from * to ** (Rnd 16 to end of pattern), completing the stuffing just before joining.
If there is a tiny gap in between the two bumps of the heart work a little stitch to close.

2. To felt both the heart and the arms, soak in reasonably hot water, then rub in a little hand soap. Wash out the soap then squeeze out the water. Rub them in between your hands: as you do this the yarn will matt together to give you the felted look you are after – if the pieces are still very damp, rub them in between a tea towel. Keep

checking the heart for shape and re-moulding if necessary. Continue rubbing and agitating until the heart and arms are quite dry and well felted, re-shaping one last time before placing on a radiator to dry.

3. Once the pieces have completely dried, sew the arms onto the heart with a matching sewing thread. Sew on the two buttons for the eyes using offcuts of the yarn and work a couple of long stitches with black sewing thread for the mouth.

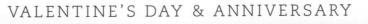

COOKIE BOUQUET
by Prudence Rogers

Delicious heart-shaped cookies, baked on sticks then dipped in chocolate, can be tied together to make a beautiful sweet bouquet for a Valentine's Day treat.

You Will Need

Heart-shaped cookie tin

Batch of cookie dough

Oven-proof cookie sticks

Vegetable oil spray

Dark cocoa and white candy melts

Chocolate transfer sheets

White chocolate and mini red heart sprinkles

Patterned ribbons

1. Lightly spray the tin with vegetable oil spray. Pat cookie dough into each heart shape until about 3mm (⅛in) below the edge. Insert cookie sticks in the indentations up to the marker line (about 5cm/2in). Bake at 180°C/350°F for about 15 minutes until firm to touch and golden brown. Allow to cool.

2. Prepare the candy melts following the manufacturer's instructions. Cover the cookies by pouring the candy melts all over; tap off the excess and place onto greaseproof paper.

3. Before the chocolate sets, cut a piece of chocolate transfer sheet to roughly the same size as the cookie and lay on top. Press down gently all over and set aside. When the chocolate has set hard, peel off the backing sheet, leaving the design on the cookie. For a variation, before the chocolate sets, sprinkle white chocolate flakes or red heart sprinkles over the cookie. Leave to set. This looks best if there is a good contrast.

4. Cut lengths of patterned ribbons to approx 30cm (12in). Tie the ribbons around the cookie sticks at the base of the hearts. Trim the ends of the ribbon at an angle with scissors.

1 HOUR

EASY PEASY

HEART FELT CARD

by Debbie Pyne

Show your love on Valentine's Day or a special anniversary with not one but three felt hearts beaded and embellished to make an extra special card.

You Will Need

White single-fold card size DL

Bright pink and pale pink felt

Pastel seed beads

Gold metallic thread

Fabric glue

1. Cut three pale pink felt hearts and two bright pink felt squares.

2. Stitch the seed beads onto the felt shapes with the gold metallic thread: use a small running stitch to sew beads around the outside of one of the hearts; work long stitches randomly over the other two hearts threading a bead onto each stitch; sew a bead to each corner of the squares with a diagonal stitch.

3. Use the heart template to draw a heart in the centre of the front of the single-fold card. Open the card and place wrong side down on a cutting mat. Cut out the marked heart using a scalpel.

4. Use fabric glue to stick the two matching embellished hearts onto the bright pink felt squares and stick onto the front of the card above and below the cut out heart.

5. Now stick the final felt heart on the inside of the card, carefully lining it up with the cut out heart on the front of the card.

1 HOUR

GET STUCK IN

Full-size templates for this project are available at: www.stitchcraftcreate.co.uk

VALENTINE'S DAY & ANNIVERSARY

CUPCAKE LOVE
by Sarah Joyce

Dark chocolate cupcakes soaked with raspberry coulis and topped with a chocolate rose swirl and piped chocolate heart – prepare to fall in love!

You Will Need

Chocolate cupcake mixture

Raspberries and raspberry coulis syrup

Chocolate buttercream icing

30g (1oz) white chocolate

Seven red cupcake wrappers

White writer icing tube

No. 2 piping nozzle

Disposable piping bags

30 MINUTES

EASY PEASY

1. Before baking the chocolate cupcakes push a raspberry into each. Once baked, brush the top of the warm cupcakes with strained raspberry coulis syrup. When completely cooled, decorate.

2. Fill a piping bag, fitted with a no. 2 piping nozzle, with the chocolate buttercream icing.

3. Starting from the centre of each cupcake, pipe a swirl to the edge to give a rose effect.

4. To make the chocolate heart decorations, melt the white chocolate in a plastic bowl by microwaving on medium power for 10-second bursts, stirring between each.

5. Use the melted chocolate to fill a piping bag fitted with PME supatube no. 2 nozzle and pipe heart shapes onto baking paper. Leave to set for 2 hours at room temperature. Once the chocolate hearts have dried completely, lift carefully and place one on the top of each cupcake. Place a fresh raspberry in the centre of each heart, and finish the cupcakes with the red wrappers.

VALENTINE'S DAY & ANNIVERSARY

ANNIVERSARY PILLOW

by Linda Clements

This pretty cushion would make a lovely anniversary memento. The couple's initials can be embroidered into one of the stitched hearts to personalize the gift.

You Will Need:

Fabric for patchwork:
Two 15.2cm (6in)
squares of pale fabric
Two 15.2cm (6in) squares
of print fabric

Dark pink fabric for borders
and backing:
Two strips 7.6cm x 26.7cm
(3in x 10½in)
Two strips 7.6cm x 39.4cm
(3in x 15½in)
One 39.4cm (15½in) square

Wadding (batting)
39.4cm (15½in) square

Pink and white stranded
cotton (floss), two buttons
and cushion pad

1. To make half square triangles, pin a pale square right sides together with a print square. Draw a line from corner to corner. Sew 6mm (¼in) on either side of the line. Cut along the line, open the two units and press seams. Repeat to make another two.

2. Check that the patchwork units are 14cm (5½in) square. Arrange the units in a windmill pattern and sew together.

3. Sew the two short borders to the patchwork and press seams outwards. Sew on the longer borders and press.

4. To quilt, use the heart and border templates and follow the template instructions. Safety pin the wadding to the back of the patchwork. Use six strands of dark pink thread to quilt the hearts on the patchwork and white thread to quilt the border design.

5. Put the backing right sides together with the front; sew 1.3cm (½in) from the edge, leaving an opening. Clip corners, turn through; press. Insert a 35.5cm (14in) pad; sew up the gap. Sew a button through the centre front and back.

1 DAY

GET STUCK IN

Full-size templates for this project are available at: www.stitchcraftcreate.co.uk

VALENTINE'S DAY & ANNIVERSARY

EASTER

BUNNY BOOKMARK
by Jayne Schofield

This cute cross stitch design is mounted onto a rectangle of pale green card to produce a pretty bookmark for an alternative Easter gift.

You Will Need

White 14-count aida

Lilac, white, pink, blue, aqua, yellow, orange and fuschia stranded cotton (floss): DMC colours 155, blanc, 3608, 824, 3846, 725, 742 and 3607

Pale green card

1 DAY

GET STUCK IN

1. Cross stitch the design onto aida with stranded cotton following the chart in the Charts section. Use two strands throughout. Trim your embroidery as marked on the chart.

2. Cut out a rectangle of green card measuring 20cm x 6.5cm (8in x 2½in). Place strips of double-sided tape on the back of your embroidery and attach it to the front of the card rectangle making sure it is central. Stick down firmly.

EASTER

BIRD'S NEST CUPCAKES

by James Brooks

Treat yourself to these delicious chocolate cupcakes decorated with buttercream nests, chirpy chicks and mini chocolate eggs.

You Will Need

One batch of chocolate cupcakes

One batch of chocolate buttercream

Disposable piping bag

Large star piping nozzle size 13

White Mexican modelling paste

Yellow, orange and black paste colours

Mini chocolate eggs

1. Take the chocolate buttercream and spoon it into a disposable piping bag fitted with a large star piping nozzle. To make the nest, pipe a ring of buttercream around the outside edge of each cupcake leaving the centre clear.

2. Now make the chicks. Colour some of the modelling paste yellow and some orange. Take a little yellow paste and roll it into a small ball to make the chick's body.

3. Take a small amount of orange paste and roll it into two cone shapes to make a beak. Stick the beak to the chick's body using a dab of water. Make as many chicks as you have cupcakes.

4. To complete the modelling paste chicks dip a cocktail stick in the black paste colour and use it to carefully dab two eyes onto each chick's face. Set the chicks aside until completely dry.

5. Place one chick and a mini chocolate egg inside the chocolate 'nest' on top of each cupcake to finish.

30 MINUTES

EASY PEASY

SPRINGTIME BIRDHOUSE
by Fiona Pearce

This wooden birdhouse embellished with springtime papers using the decoupage technique makes a beautiful decoration or table centrepiece.

You Will Need

Birdhouse blank

Patterned paper

Decoupage glue

Ribbon

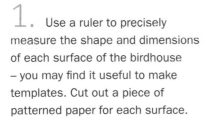

1. Use a ruler to precisely measure the shape and dimensions of each surface of the birdhouse – you may find it useful to make templates. Cut out a piece of patterned paper for each surface.

2. Apply decoupage glue to the area to be covered, then gently smooth the paper onto the surface with your fingers, pressing firmly to remove any air bubbles. Wipe away excess glue with a damp cloth.

3. Once each surface of the birdhouse is covered with paper, apply another two coats of decoupage glue over all of the paper surfaces, allowing each coat to dry before adding the next.

4. When the paper has completely dried, use a craft knife to cut out the hole on the front of the birdhouse. Trim the edges of the roof with the ribbon using craft glue to attach it. If you wish, you can add other embellishments too, cutting motifs from patterned papers for example, or using springtime-themed stickers. *Please note that the birdhouse is not waterproof and should not be left outside.*

1 HOUR

EASY PEASY

EASTER

KNITTED EASTER BUNNY
by Claire Garland

This cute knitted bunny toy is the perfect Easter accessory and will be sure to melt the hearts of anyone who sees him.

You Will Need

Set 3.5mm (US size 4) double-pointed needles

1 x 50g ball Patons Wool Blend DK dark grey plus small amount of cream

Toy filling

Gold felt

Pink and black sewing thread

Pompom making set

Ribbon

2 HOURS

FANCY A CHALLENGE

1. Knit the bunny following the pattern below:

Ears
For the first ear:
*Cast on 6sts onto one needle then complete the cast on as follows:
Step 1: Hold needle with sts in LH.

Step 2: Hold 2 empty dpns parallel in RH.
Step 3: Slip 1st cast on st purlwise onto the dpn closest to you and off the needle in the LH, then slip the next cast on st onto the dpn furthest away and off the RH needle. Repeat step 3 until all 6sts are divided onto the 2 parallel dpns, 3sts on front dpn and 3sts on back. Slide sts to the other ends of the dpns, working yarn at back.
RS facing, cont working in the rnd, beginning by knitting the sts on the back dpn – work sts over 2 dpns, using a 3rd dpn to knit with:

Rnd 1: K6.
Rep last rnd 14 times.**
Break yarn and leave sts on needles.
For the second ear:
Work as first ear from * to **.
To join both ears:
Rnd 16: K3 across front of second ear, k3 across front of first ear – all onto one dpn, k3 across back of first ear, k3 across back of second ear – all onto a second dpn. 12sts

Begin head
Rnd 17: (inc) Kf&b, k4, kf&b, kf&b, k4, kf&b. 16sts (8sts each needle)
Place marker.

Rnd 18: K16.

Rnd 19: (inc) Kf&b, k3, m1, k3, kf&b (across the front of the head), kf&b, k6, kf&b (across the back of the head). 21sts

Rnds 21, 23, 25: K.

Rnd 22: (inc) K5, kf&b, k5, k10. 22sts

Rnd 24: (inc) K6, m1, k6, k10. 23sts

Rnd 26: (inc) K6, kf&b, k6, k10. 24sts

Rnd 27: K24.

Rep last rnd three times more.

Shape chin/neck

Rnd 31: (dec) [Sl1, kl, psso, k2twice, k2tog, k2, k2tog, k10. 20sts

Rnd 32: K20.

Rnd 33: (dec) Sl1, kl, psso, k6, k2tog, sl1, kl, psso, k6, k2tog. 16sts

Rnd 34: K16.

Rep last rnd twice more.

Shape front

Rnd 37: (inc) K4, m1, k4, k8. 17sts

Rnds 38, 40, 42, 44, 46, 48, 50: K.

Rnd 39: (inc) K4, kf&b, k4, k8. 18sts

Rnd 41: (inc) K5, m1, k5, k4, m1, k4. 20sts

Rnd 43: (inc) K5, kf&b, k5, k4, kf&b, k4. 22sts

Rnd 45: (inc) K6, m1, k6, k5, m1, k5. 24sts

Rnd 47: (inc) K6, kf&b, k6, k5, kf&b, k5. 26sts

Rnd 49: (inc) K7, m1, k7, k6, m1, k6. 28sts

Rnd 51: (inc) K7, kf&b, k7, k6, kf&b, k6. 30sts

Rnd 52: K30.

Rep last rnd 10 times.

Rnd 63: (dec) Sl1, kl, psso, 12, k2tog, k14. 28sts

Legs

First leg:

Rnd 64: K7, slip the next 7sts off the needle and onto a safety pin, slip next 7 sts (from back needle) off the needle and onto another safety pin, knit next 7 sts onto a second dpn – 7sts on one needle, 7sts on the other. Place marker.

*Rnd 65: K14.

Rep last rnd 9 times.

Foot:

Rnd 75: (inc) K3, kf&b, k3, k7. 15sts

Rnds 76, 78, 80: K.

Rnd 77: (inc) K4, m1, k4, k7. 16sts

Rnd 79: (inc) K4, kf&b, k4, k7. 17sts

Rnd 81: (inc) K5, m1, k5, k7. 18sts

Rnd 82: K18.

Rep last rnd 10 times.

Rnd 93: (dec) Sl1, kl, psso, k7, k2tog, k7. 16sts

Rnd 94: K16.

Rnd 95: (dec) Sl1, kl, psso, k5, k2tog, k7. 14sts**

Cut yarn leaving 10cm (4in) tail. Finish seam using grafting technique. Stuff the body, leg and foot.

Second leg:

Slip 2 sets of 7sts that are held on the safety pins onto 2 dpns. With front of the bunny facing you rejoin yarn to first set of 7sts and work the second leg as the first from * to **. Stuff the leg and foot. Cut yarn leaving 10cm (4in) tail. Finish seam using grafting technique. If there is a gap between the legs, work a couple of sts to close it.

Arms (make 2)

Leaving a long tail end (to sew the arm to the body later), cast on 8sts onto one needle then complete the cast on using the same method used for the ears.

Rnd 1: K8. Place marker.

Rep last rnd 10 times.

Rnd 12: (inc) K2, m1, k2, k4. 9sts

Rnds 13, 15, 17, 19, 21, 23, 25, 27: K.

Rnd 14: (inc) K2, kf&b, k2, k4. 10sts

Rnd 16: (inc) K3, m1, k3, k4. 11sts

Rnd 18: (inc) K3, kf&b, k3, k4. 12sts

Rnd 20: (inc) K4, m1, k4, k4. 13sts

Rnd 22: (inc) K4, kf&b, k4, k4. 14sts

Rnd 24: (dec) Sl1, kl, psso, k6, k2tog, k4. 12sts

Rnd 26: (dec) Sl1, kl, psso, k4, k2tog, k4. 10sts

Rnd 28: (dec) Sl1, kl, psso, k2, k2tog, k4. 8sts

Stuff the arm.

Cut yarn, thread end through rem 8sts, pull up tight and secure. Join the arms to the sides of the body using the tail ends.

2. Work the facial details. For the nose, sew a few straight lines in pink. For the mouth, sew two single straight lines in an upside down T-shape in black. To form the eyes, work a few small stitches in black, over and over, symmetrically on either side of the head.

3. Make a bobtail from cream yarn using the smaller of the pompom templates and sew in place on the back of the toy. Cut out an oval shape from gold felt and sew onto the front, working small horizontal stitches around the edge of the tummy.

'TREE OF LIFE' CARD
by Charlotte Addison

This sweet little Easter card has a pretty tree design that is decorated with a lovely range of embroidered brads.

You Will Need

Patterned paper

Cream single-fold card size C6

Embroidered brads

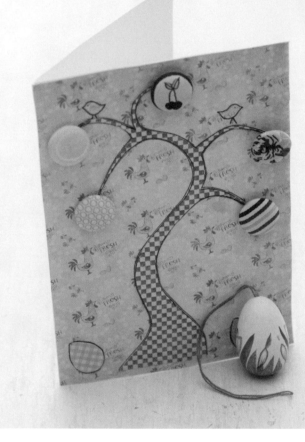

1. Cut out a piece of patterned paper measuring 14.8cm x 10.5cm (6in x 4in) to fit the front of the single-fold card. Using the template, cut out a tree from contrasting paper and stick to the front of the paper panel.

2. Attach the embroidered brads to the end of the tree branches. Embellish your design with paper eggs and draw on some chicks to sit on the branches. Stick the decorated panel to the front of the single-fold card.

1 HOUR

EASY PEASY

Full-size templates for this project are available at: www.stitchcraftcreate.co.uk

EASTER

CUTE EGG COSIES
by Ellen Kharade

These egg cosies are perfect for the Easter breakfast table. Instructions are given for making the bunny cosy but you can easily adapt these to make the alternative designs.

You Will Need

Small pieces of white felt and patterned fabric

Narrow flower braid, ric rac and ribbon

Lightweight wadding (batting)

Scrap of fusible webbing

Brown and pink stranded cotton (floss)

2 HOURS

GET STUCK IN

1. Use the bunny cosy template to cut three pieces of patterned fabric and two pieces of wadding. Use the bunny body template to cut one piece of patterned fabric. Use the bunny face template to cut one piece of white felt. Pin the curved edges of the face to the body, right sides facing; machine stitch. Hand sew ric rac across the middle of the patterned fabric, and flower braid across the fabric change. Sew on the bunny's facial details.

2. Iron a small piece of fusible webbing to the back of a small piece of the patterned fabric, then use the ear template to cut out two inner ear pieces. Cut two outer ear pieces from white felt. Iron the inner ear pieces in place on the outer ear pieces and machine stitch in place. Tack (baste) the ears to the top of the bunny cosy front, with right sides facing and ears pointing downwards. Pin front and back together, right sides facing.

3. Machine stitch all around leaving the bottom edge open. Sandwich the lining pieces (right sides facing) between the wadding pieces. Pin, then machine sew to leave bottom edge open. Turn lining through to the right side, push into the cosy shell (right sides facing) and pin. Machine sew along one side of the bottom edge. Turn the right way out, push the lining into the cosy, and sew along the other side. Hand sew ribbon around the bottom edge.

Full-size templates for this project are available at: www.stitchcraftcreate.co.uk

EASTER

PAPER BEAD BRACELETS
by Danielle Lowy

As an alternative to chocolate or sweets, give these handmade bracelets as a unique Easter gift. The cute egg-shaped beads and pretty pastel colours will delight all ages!

You Will Need

Sheets of patterned paper
15cm x 15cm (6in x 6in)

Seed beads

Elastic cord

Sealing varnish

Foam block and
cocktail sticks

1. Each bead is made from a long triangle of paper. First mark out the triangles onto the back of your paper sheets: make a pencil mark every 2cm (¾in) down the right-hand side; on the left-hand side, make the first mark at 1cm (⅜in), then all subsequent marks 2cm (¾in) apart.

2. To join the pencil marks, draw a line from the top right hand corner to the 1cm (⅜in) mark on the left-hand side, then draw a line from the 1cm (⅜in) mark to the first 2cm (¾in) mark on the right-hand side, and carry on zigzagging down the sheet.

3. Cut the triangles out, discarding those marked first and last on the paper sheet. Take a paper triangle and starting at the wide end, roll it snugly round a cocktail stick. Glue the last 10cm (4in) to keep the paper from unfurling, then place the cocktail stick in a foam block. Make nine more beads in the same way.

4. Apply a coat of sealing varnish to the beads and leave to dry; then apply another coat of varnish to ensure strong shiny beads. When dry, twist the beads off the cocktail sticks.

5. Cut a 30cm (12in) length of elastic cord and attach a paper clip about 5cm (2in) from one end. Thread on paper beads interspersed with seed beads – the number required will depend on the wrist size. Remove the paper clip and tie the ends together tightly in a knot. Cut off excess cord.

1 HOUR

EASY PEASY

EASTER

EASTER EGG GIFT BAG
by Mary Fogg

This pretty gift bag is the perfect way to present lots of delicious Easter treats – simply fill with chocolate eggs and pull the drawstrings tight.

You Will Need

Fabric for main bag:
Two pieces floral fabric
40cm x 40cm (15¾in x 15¾in)
Two pieces gingham fabric
17cm x 40cm (6¾in x 15¾in)

Fabric for lining:
Two pieces gingham fabric
40cm x 57cm (15¾in x 22½in)

Fabric for drawstrings:
Two pieces floral fabric
90cm x 6cm (35½in x 2⅜in)

Small piece of gingham
fabric for appliqué

Fusible webbing

Ribbon and button

1. To make the bag front, line a piece of gingham fabric up with a floral fabric piece, right sides facing. Pin then sew along the top edge with a 6mm (¼in) seam allowance; press. Repeat for the bag back.

2. Cut the egg from gingham fabric. Sew ribbon horizontally along its centre. Attach to the bag front using fusible webbing. Sew on the button and blanket stitch around the appliqué design.

3. Place bag front and back together, right sides facing; pin then machine stitch, stopping 6cm (2⅜in) from the top on either side. Place the two lining fabric pieces together, right sides facing. Pin then machine stitch all the way to the top on both sides. Turn the main bag through to the right side and press. Topstitch down each side and across the bottom of the opening at the top of the bag. Turn over and press a 2cm (¾in) hem along both the top edge of the bag and the lining.

4. Place lining inside bag (wrong sides facing); pin top edge matching hems; topstitch. Repeat 2cm (¾in) below for drawstring channel. Press 1cm (⅜in) hem on floral fabric strips; fold so hems meet and sew. Thread drawstrings through and knot ends.

2 HOURS

FANCY A CHALLENGE

Full-size templates for this project are available at: www.stitchcraftcreate.co.uk

EASTER

TREAT BASKETS
by Marion Elliot

These little baskets made from double-sided patterned papers are perfectly pretty containers for chocolate eggs and other sweet treats.

You Will Need

Double-sided paper pack
30cm x 30cm (12in x 12in)

Lace edge paper punch

1. First decide which side of the paper you want as the inside of your basket. Trace and transfer the Easter basket template onto this side of the paper.

2. Cut the basket out, then score along the fold lines as marked on the template. Fold up the sides and tabs to make the basket shape. Glue the tabs in place taking care not to use too much glue.

3. To make the basket handle cut a 1.5cm (⅝in) wide strip of contrasting paper. Trim to the desired length and stick to the outside top edge of the box.

4. Use the lace edge paper punch along one edge of another sheet of contrasting paper. Cut off the decorative strip and trim so that the length fits around the top of the basket, allowing for an overlap.

5. Glue the paper lace strip in place around the outside rim of the basket, covering the join for the ends of the handle.

30 MINUTES

GET STUCK IN

Full-size templates for this project are available at: www.stitchcraftcreate.co.uk

EASTER

BUNNY BISCUITS
by Ruth Clemens

These cute bunny biscuits are perfect for an Easter party.
Practise your royal icing skills to master this project.

You Will Need

Six circular biscuits

White sugarpaste

White sugar florist
paste (SFP)

Brown, green and blue
gel paste colours

Royal icing

Black icing pen

Disposable piping bags

No. 1, 2 and 3 piping nozzles

Fluted circle cutter
5.5cm (2¼in) diameter

1. Knead together equal amounts of white sugarpaste and white SFP. Colour the paste a pale blue using gel paste colouring. Roll out the blue paste to 2mm (³⁄₃₂in) thick. Cut out six fluted circles and set aside to dry. Once dry, prepare the royal icing. Colour one third brown and one third green. Put the green royal icing in a piping bag fitted with a no. 1 nozzle and the remaining white in a bag fitted with a no. 2 nozzle. Add a drop of water to loosen the brown royal icing and add to a piping bag fitted with a no. 3 nozzle.

2. Decorate the circles: allow each piped part to dry slightly before adding the next to avoid bleeding.
For the feet: pipe two brown teardrops, one third of the way up.
For the body: pipe a 1.5cm (⅝in) bulb just above the feet.
For the head: pipe a 1cm (⅜in) bulb.
For the ears: pipe two teardrops, flopping one over slightly.
For the grass: use green either side.
For the whiskers: use black icing pen to draw onto either side of the head.
For the bobtail: add a small bulb of white to base of body.

3. Allow the royal icing to dry completely before securing each disc to the top of each biscuit using a light brush of water.

1 HOUR

FANCY A
CHALLENGE

SPRINGTIME ROSETTES
by Zoe Larkins

Use these paper rosettes to decorate your Easter gifts or to reward the best egg hunter. They have a handy folded card on the front for a special message.

You Will Need

Heavyweight patterned paper

Cream card

Easter-themed stickers

String

1. Cut a rectangle measuring 20cm x 10cm (8in x 4in) from the patterned paper. Using a bone folder, score lines across the 20cm length at 1cm (⅜in) intervals, working from top to bottom.

2. Carefully fold each scored line in alternate directions to give you a concertina-folded piece of paper. Measure to the middle point (5cm/2in), fold in half and tie a piece of string around the centre to secure.

3. Bring the top and bottom edges together at each side to make a circle, and staple the edges together.

4. Fold a piece of cream card in half to write your Easter message inside. Embellish the front of the card with an Easter-themed sticker then carefully cut around the outline of the sticker, taking care not to cut through the folded edge. Glue to the centre of your rosette.

5. To form the rosette tails cut a strip of card measuring 20cm x 2cm (8in x ¾in). Fold in half at a slight angle, and trim the ends into points. Glue onto the back of the rosette.

30 MINUTES

EASY PEASY

EASTER

PRETTY EGG GARLAND
by Charlotte Addison

Create a cute fabric egg garland to decorate your home at Easter. Make the garland as long as you require by simply adding more eggs!

You Will Need

Pink and blue patterned fabrics

Wadding (batting)

1m (40in) white cord

1m (40in) cream ric rac

Flower-shaped buttons

1–2 HOURS

GET STUCK IN

1. Using the template, cut six egg shapes from both the pink and the blue patterned fabrics and six from the wadding.

2. Sandwich a wadding egg between a pink and blue fabric egg, right sides facing out. Pin ric rac around the edge of the egg, then use a machine zigzag stitch to secure the ric rac in place. Repeat to complete all six eggs.

3. Use a needle to thread the white cord through the top of the fabric eggs, knotting the cord at either side to secure the eggs in place (if you don't want them to move around on the cord). Tie loops at either end of the cord so that the garland can be hung up.

4. Sew a flower-shaped button to the front of each of the eggs (centre top) to finish.

Full-size templates for this project are available at: www.stitchcraftcreate.co.uk

EASTER

MOTHER'S DAY
&
FATHER'S DAY

HAPPY PHOTO HOOP
by Jennifer Grace

Make a picture to treasure by decorating an embroidery hoop with a family photo framed with patterned papers – a great keepsake for Mother's or Father's Day.

You Will Need

Embroidery hoop
20cm (10in) diameter

Gold metallic crochet thread

White linen fabric

Photograph

Patterned papers

Small flower punches

Brads and buttons

3 HOURS

EASY PEASY

1. Put a drop of hot glue at the top back of the outer circle of the embroidery hoop, and attach the end of the gold thread. Spiral the crochet thread around the hoop to neatly cover it, adding another drop of glue to secure it when you get back to the start.

2. Place the linen fabric into the hoop, stretching it out and tightening the hoop.

3. Trim your photograph to 13cm x 10cm (5in x 4in). Choose five patterned papers to match the colours in the photograph. Use double-sided tape to attach your photograph to a piece of patterned paper measuring 15cm x 13cm (6in x 5in), then attach this in turn to a piece of contrasting patterned paper measuring 15cm (6in) square. Use hot glue to adhere the layered panel so that it is slightly off centre on the hoop.

4. Punch lots of flowers from the other three sheets of patterned paper and attach to opposite corners of the photo panel, again using hot glue. Use a paper piercer to make some holes to fit the brads through the fabric. Use a hot glue gun to attach a scattering of small buttons. Trim away any excess material at the back of your hoop.

MOTHER'S DAY & FATHER'S DAY

DAISY BUTTON CUPCAKES
by Fiona Pearce

These pretty cupcakes, each decorated with three large daisies
with button centres, are great for Mother's Day.

You Will Need

One batch of
vanilla cupcakes

White and pink sugar
florist paste (SFP)

White and pale
green sugarpaste

Circle, large daisy and
small leaf plunger cutters

Silicone button mould

Edible glue

30 MINUTES

EASY PEASY

1. Roll out some white SFP
finely on a non-stick surface.
Use the daisy cutter to cut out
three flowers for each cupcake.

2. Place the flowers into an
empty egg carton to mould them into
their distinctive cupped shape. Leave
the flowers to dry so that they hold
their shape.

3. Roll out some green
sugarpaste to 2mm (³⁄₃₂in) thick. Use
the small leaf plunger cutter to cut
out three leaves for each cupcake,
pushing the plunger down to imprint
veins into the leaf. Pinch the base
of each leaf into a 'V' shape.

4. Press some pink SFP into
a silicone button mould to make
three buttons for each cupcake.

5. Attach the buttons into the
centre of each flower using edible
glue applied with a fine paintbrush.
Cover the top of each cupcake
with a circle of white sugarpaste
that has been rolled out to 3mm
(¹⁄₈in) thick. Attach the flowers
and the leaves to the centre of
the cupcakes using edible glue.

HEARTS GARLAND
by Mary Fogg

This shabby chic garland of hearts stuffed with sweet-smelling lavender makes a lovely gift for Mother's Day. This project is great for using up fabric leftovers.

You Will Need

Fabric for hearts: Five pieces printed cotton 30cm x 21cm (11¾in x 8¼in)

Dried lavender

Toy filling

Pink ribbon

2 HOURS

GET STUCK IN

1. Make a heart template from card. Take one piece of your chosen fabric and fold in half, short sides together with right sides facing, and pin. Use the card template and a pencil to draw the heart shape onto the fabric. Starting three-quarters along one side of the heart shape, stitch carefully around the marked line leaving a 5cm (2in) gap for turning. Repeat for each piece of fabric.

2. Cut out the heart shapes 6mm (¼in) from the sewing line. Carefully snip into the curves and down into the 'V' of the heart shape. Turn each heart right side out, and gently press into shape.

3. Stuff each heart with toy filling and add a generous scoop of lavender before slip stitching the opening closed.

4. Stitch a ribbon bow onto the front of each heart. Making sure the hearts are right sides facing, securely stitch them together at their widest point to form a chain.

5. Cut two lengths of ribbon and stitch one piece at either end of your chain of hearts.

Full-size templates for this project are available at: www.stitchcraftcreate.co.uk

MOTHER'S DAY & FATHER'S DAY

TEAM COLOUR CAKES
by Prudence Rogers

These cool football and rugby mini cakes are a fun Father's Day treat for a sports-obsessed dad. Personalize them with his team's colours.

You Will Need

One batch of vanilla mini cake sponges and one batch of buttercream icing

10cm (4in) diameter cake cards

White sugarpaste and green food colouring

Red, black and brown gel paste colours

No. 233 grass piping nozzle

2 HOURS

GET STUCK IN

1. Colour a portion of sugarpaste green, roll out thinly; use to cover the cake cards with a drop of water.

2. For the scarf design cover the mini cake evenly with buttercream icing and chill to firm. Roll out white sugarpaste to 5mm (³⁄₁₆in) thick and cover the cake, working the icing around the sides with your hands; trim away excess. Use a dab of royal icing to stick the cake to the card.

3. Cut out six hexagons from 3mm (1⅛in) thick black sugarpaste; apply in an evenly spaced pattern to the cake top with a little water. Make red and white sugarpaste sausages 5cm (2in) long by 1.5cm (⅝in) wide. Arrange next to each other so they are touching, alternating the colours. Roll out to 5mm (³⁄₁₆in) thick so the colours join to make stripes. Cut a rectangle 3mm (⅛in) taller than the cake height, and 5cm (2in) less than the cake's circumference.

4. Roll red/blue and white sugarpaste balls; add to the scarf end with water. Squeeze more sugarpaste through a sugarcraft extruder gun for tassels. Bunch up at one end and join to the balls.

5. For the sports field design pipe green buttercream all over the cake. Roll a brown sugarpaste rugby ball, indent seams and use white sugarpaste for the stitching.

Full-size templates for this project are available at: www.stitchcraftcreate.co.uk

MOTHER'S DAY & FATHER'S DAY

SCALLOPED CIRCLES CARD
by Jane Millard

This stylish card for Father's Day is decorated with layered scalloped circles and chipboard embellishments.

You Will Need

Co-ordinating patterned papers

Single-fold card 13.5cm x 13.5cm (5¼in x 5¼in)

Scalloped circle punch

Chipboard strips and brad embellishment

30 MINUTES

EASY PEASY

1. Cut a piece of dark patterned paper measuring 13cm x 13cm (5in x 5in). Cut a piece of lighter patterned paper measuring 12.5cm x 12.5cm (4⅞in x 4⅞in).

2. Punch 18 circles and layer onto the smaller piece of patterned paper overlapping until you have built up four rows. Trim the edges to fit the square. Add chipboard strips trimmed to size to neaten top row.

3. Add the brad embellishment to the top right-hand corner. Add the finished panel to the dark patterned paper square and attach to the front of the single-fold card.

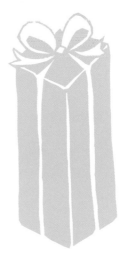

PAPER PINWHEEL CARD
by Jane Millard

This pretty 3D card with a paper pinwheel and punched flowers
is just perfect for a special Mother's Day greeting.

You Will Need

Co-ordinating
patterned papers

Double-sided
patterned paper

White single-fold
card 13.5cm x 13.5cm
(5¼in x 5¼in)

Flat-backed pearls
and pink brad

Cocktail stick

Very thin ribbon

Flower punch

1. Cut a piece of blue patterned paper measuring 13cm x 13cm (5in x 5in). Cut a strip of green paper measuring 13cm x 3cm (5in x 1⅛in); trim along one edge with pinking scissors. Machine stitch the 'grass' strip to the base of the blue paper panel.

2. To make the pinwheel, cut a piece of double-sided paper measuring 6cm x 6cm (2⅜in x 2⅜in) and draw a cross diagonally on the wrong side from corner to corner.

3. Make a hole in the centre of the cross and on each alternate point. Fold the points to the centre, and fix with the brad. Attach to the cocktail stick with hot glue. Tie ribbon around the pinwheel handle and tuck under the grass strip.

4. Glue the embellished panel onto the front of the single-fold card. Punch flowers from patterned papers and attach to the grass strip, adding a flat-backed pearl to the centre of each.

30 MINUTES

GET STUCK IN

HANDY POCKET TIDY

by Linda Clements

This fabric box makes a great Father's Day present, giving dad somewhere to store his pocket contents tidily until morning.

You Will Need:

Dark print fabric:
Three strips 4.4cm x 61cm
(1¾in x 24in)

Medium print fabric:
Three strips
4.4cm x 61cm (1¾in x 24in)

Light print fabric:
Three strips 4.4cm x 61cm
(1¾in x 24in)

Wadding (batting)
28cm (11in) square

Sewing threads and
red quilting thread

Four buttons

1. Using 6mm (¼in) seams, sew the strips together, alternating the colours: dark, medium, light. Press seams. Cut the unit into two squares each 29.8cm (11¾in).

2. Safety pin the wadding to the back of one of the patchwork squares, leaving the seam allowance free. Pin the other square right sides together with the first square, aligning all edges. Sew together all round leaving a gap for turning.

3. Clip corners, turn through. Sew the gap up and press. With matching thread, topstitch around 3mm (⅛in) from the edge. Quilt the patchwork using red thread and any pattern you like.

4. Press all sides in by 5cm (2in), pressing firmly to crease the base. Take each corner in turn and pinch the two top edges together so the sides are vertical. Using matching thread, stitch through the two edges, 5cm (2in) in from each corner, to fix the corner. Press the flap of fabric inwards, to make a kite shape, and sew a button in position. Repeat on all four corners.

4 HOURS

GET STUCK IN

PRETTY STORAGE POCKETS
by Rosina Cassam

This attractive cover transforms an ordinary clothes hanger into a practical storage unit. The perfect Mother's Day gift, use it to keep fashion accessories to hand.

You Will Need

Patterned fabric

Plain fabric

Wire hanger

1 HOUR

FANCY A CHALLENGE

1. To make your pattern, trace around the top of the wire hanger and lengthen to about 30cm (12in). Add a 1cm (⅜in) seam allowance all around. This is the hanger cover pattern. To make the pocket pattern, fold over the top part of the hanger cover pattern to use the lower part only (about 20cm/8in deep).

2. Transfer the pattern pieces to your fabric. Cut two main hanger cover pieces from patterned fabric and two lining pieces from plain fabric. Cut one main pocket piece from patterned fabric and one lining from plain fabric.

3. Place the pocket pieces together with right sides facing and machine sew along the top edge. Turn through to the right side and press flat.

4. Place one of the main hanger cover pieces right side up on your work surface and lay the pocket on top with the lining facing down, taking care to align the raw edges at the bottom edge. Sew along the pocket sides and bottom edge. Measure 13cm (5in) in from the sides to mark the pocket divisions and machine stitch to make three pockets.

5. Place the hanger cover lining on top of the (pocket) front right sides facing, and machine sew along bottom edge only. Press; fold open along seam edge and press. Repeat with the remaining fabric pieces to make the hanger cover back. Pin the linings to the hanger cover pieces and sew around the top edges.

6. Place the lined back and front together, right sides facing, and sew along the top edge, leaving a 5cm (2in) gap. Turn right side out and press flat along the seams. Insert the hanger through the gap and hang up ready to use.

MOTHER'S DAY & FATHER'S DAY

STRIPED LAP QUILT
by Linda Clements

This quilt is easy to make for a special Mother's Day gift. You could add more strips to make it into a single-bed quilt or use blues, browns and greens for a Father's Day present.

You Will Need:

Five prints: 0.25m (¼yd) of each cut into two strips 12.7cm x 111.8cm (5in x 44in)

White backing fabric 1.6m (1¾yd) 106.7cm (42in) wide

Wadding (batting) 127cm (50in) square

Sewing and quilting threads

1 DAY   GET STUCK IN

1. Arrange the strips and sew together along the long sides using 6mm (¼in) seams and press. Trim so edges are straight. Cut wadding (batting) slightly larger and safety pin it to the back of the quilt, with layers flat. Machine or hand quilt 1.3cm (½in) away from each seam.

2. Remove pins, press and trim the wadding so that it is flush with the quilt.

3. Prepare backing fabric so it's 5cm (2in) larger than the quilt all round. Place backing right side down and quilt right side up on top, with a border of backing all around. Safety pin the layers together.

4. Do further quilting 1.3cm (½in) away from the previous quilting lines. Remove pins and press. Pull the quilting thread ends through to the front of the quilt.

5. Trim the backing so it's 2.5cm (1in) larger than the quilt all round. Working one side at a time, fold the backing over by 1.3cm (½in) and then again, on to the quilt front. Pin in place and machine sew 3mm (⅛in) from the edge of the binding. Repeat on all sides and press.

WEDDING

HANGING HEARTS
by Jenny Arnott

These sweet fabric hearts, filled with scented lavender, would make lovely fragrant wedding favours or gifts for the bridal party.

You Will Need

Floral patterned fabrics

Ribbons

Buttons

Dried lavender

1 HOUR

GET STUCK IN

1. For each heart, cut two fabric heart shapes from floral fabric.

2. Cut a length of ribbon 13cm (5in) long and fold in half. Sandwich the ribbon with loop facing down between the front and back heart pieces (right sides together) at the top edge. Machine stitch all around the heart with a 5mm (³⁄₁₆in) seam allowance, leaving a 4cm (1½in) gap open along one side. Clip the curves, then turn the heart right side out.

3. Press well before filling the the heart with scented lavender. Sew the opening closed with neat hand stitches and matching thread. Add a decorative button at the base of the ribbon to finish.

Full-size templates for this project are available at: www.stitchcraftcreate.co.uk

WEDDING

PAPER ROSE BOUQUET
by Dorothy Wood

This beautiful bridal bouquet will last forever. The paper roses are made from patterned paper and assembled with wire, then tied together with loops of ribbon.

You Will Need

30 sheets of co-ordinating patterned papers 15cm x 15cm (6in x 6in)

Ribbons in varying widths

Silver wire

Ultra-adhesive tape

Distress ink

Embossing tool

3 HOURS

FANCY A CHALLENGE

1. Trace off the petal templates and cut out from stiff card. Arrange the papers in six bundles, each containing five sheets (one for each rose). Draw around all three petal templates onto each paper bundle. Holding the papers together firmly, cut out the petals from each bundle.

2. Dab the petal edges with the ink. Crumple up each petal to distress the paper.

3. Run a large embossing tool around the top edge of each petal on the reverse side of the centre point. Repeat for all 15 petals to make a single rose. Pull top edges over closed scissors to curl further. Roll a small petal around a pencil to create a cone shape with the petal curving out at the top. Tape to secure and remove the pencil. Add the other small petals one at a time covering the join of the previous petal each time.

4. Fold 50cm (20in) of wire in half and twist stem; tuck cut end into rose. Add the medium petals taping each in position. Add the large petals allowing them to bloom out to create a rose. Wrap loops of ribbon with wire and leave tail as stem. Wrap rose and ribbon stems with ultra-adhesive tape and assemble the bouquet wrapping with wire. Cover a card tube, and stick over the stems. Tie ribbon to create long tails at top of handle.

Full-size templates for this project are available at: www.stitchcraftcreate.co.uk

WEDDING

LACY HEART CUPCAKES
by Fiona Pearce

Individually made cupcakes make a great alternative to a formal wedding cake. These have a lovely stitched pattern and are decorated with blossoms formed into a heart.

You Will Need

One batch of cupcakes

White and pale pink sugarpaste

White royal icing

Disposable piping bag

No. 2 piping nozzle

Quilting tool

Small blossom plunger cutter

Circle cutter

Edible glue

Lacy cupcake wrappers

Foam mat

Ball modelling tool

1. Roll out the white sugarpaste to 3mm (⅛in) thick. Use the circle cutter to cut circles from it. Use the palm of your hand to smooth each circle into position on top of the cakes; use the quilting tool to imprint the criss-cross pattern.

2. Roll out the pink sugarpaste to 2mm (³⁄₃₂in) thick. Use the blossom plunger cutter to cut 16 small blossoms for each cupcake.

3. Place the small pale pink blossoms onto a foam mat. Gently press the small end of a ball modelling tool into the centre of the blossoms to give each of them a lovely cupped shape.

4. Arrange the cupped blossoms on top of each cupcake to form a heart shape, using edible glue applied with a fine paintbrush to hold them in place.

5. Pipe a small dot of white royal icing into the centre of each blossom using a piping bag fitted with a no. 2 nozzle. Place the cupcakes into the cupcake wrappers to finish.

1 HOUR

EASY PEASY

WEDDING CUFF BRACLET
by Dorothy Wood

A sparkly bracelet made with beautiful white crystal beads makes the perfect bridesmaids' gift.

You Will Need

White crystal bead pack including seed beads, bugles and pearls

Swarovski crystal rainbow beads

Beading thread and size 10 beading needle

Silver slider clasp with five holes

3 HOURS

FANCY A CHALLENGE

1. Secure a 2.5m (2¾yd) length of beading thread to the bottom loop of one part of the slider clasp. Pick up 3cm (1⅛in) of seed beads and bugles in a random order and feed the tail through the beads too.

2. Pick up a Swarovskl crystal bead then another 3cm (1⅛in) of the white crystal beads, then a Swarovski crystal. Repeat three times to make a 16cm (6¼in) string, adding a small pearl on one section.

3. Sew twice through the bottom loop on the other part of the slider clasp. Add 3cm (1⅛in) of beads (including a small pearl), a crystal and 3cm (1⅛in) of beads. Pass the needle through the crystal on the strand below. Continue adding beads and passing the needle through every second crystal.

4. Add 3cm (1⅛in) beads to reach the second loop. Sew twice through the loop, go back through

the first seed bead. Work back along taking the needle through every second crystal on the row below, occasionally adding small and large pearls amongst the seed beads.

5. On reaching the last loop, sew round it twice going back through several beads. Sew a half hitch knot around the main thread between two beads. Go through a few more beads and repeat before trimming the tail. Secure knots with glue.

PRETTY FAVOUR WRAPS
by Chloe Adcock

It is quick to make your own pretty paper wedding favour wraps and you can easily complete 50 in a day. The punched aperture reveals the treat in store.

You Will Need

Sheets of patterned paper 30cm x 30cm (12in x 12in)

Cellophane bags size C6

Scalloped square punch

Glitter pens

10 MINUTES

EASY PEASY

1. Cut a sheet of paper into three strips measuring 10cm (4in) wide. Take one strip and score two lines 13.5cm (5½in) from each of the short sides, creating a 2.5cm (1in) wide strip in the centre, which will form the base. Fold the score lines to create the front, base and back of the wrap.

2. Use the scalloped square punch to punch an aperture in the front panel 2.5cm (1in) from the base. (Keep the punched out shape to hide the staples once the cellophane bag is sealed later.)

3. Cut a 2cm (¾in) wide strip of co-ordinating paper. Trim 10cm (4in) from one end and set aside. Use glitter pens to draw a dashed line along one side of the remaining paper strip. Concertina-fold, then stick the two ends together, and flatten to create a rosette. Cut a circular piece of co-ordinating paper, edge with glitter pens and adhere to the centre of the rosette.

4. Cut out a label shape and adhere it and the rosette to the set-aside 10cm (4in) strip. Add the guest's name to the label.

5. Cut the top from a C6 cellophane bag and fill with sweets. Fold over the top and staple the sweets pouch into position through the paper wrap. Conceal the staples front and back with the embellishments.

WEDDING

BRIDE AND GROOM CAKES
by James Brooks

These push pop cakes, with their top hat and bridal rose toppers,
would be perfect for wedding favours or sweet table displays.

You Will Need

Half batch vanilla cupcakes

Half batch chocolate cupcakes

One batch buttercream

White Mexican modelling paste

Pink and black paste colours

Pink candy food dust

Cake push pop holders

Disposable piping bag

1. Assemble the push pops. Colour buttercream pink, spoon into the piping bag and snip off the end. For the bride push pops, cut two circles from vanilla cupcakes using a push pop tube and top each with a simple swirl of pink buttercream. Repeat for the groom push pops using the chocolate cupcakes.

2. To make the top hat: add black paste colour to white modelling paste to make silver-grey. Roll out a little and use a push pop tube to cut a circle for the hat base.

3. Roll out a paste sausage smaller than the circle; cut off a 2.5cm (1in) segment, ensuring both ends remain perfectly flat. Stick to the circle with a dab of water; set aside to dry. Complete the top hat by adding a thin ribbon of pink-coloured modelling paste around the base of the hat.

4. To make the rose, cut out four circles from rolled out white modelling paste. Smooth the top edge of each circle with your thumb to form the edges of the petals.

5. Roll one petal closed, with the thin edge at the top, to form the centre of the rose. Roll the three remaining petals around this. Set aside to dry, then place the top hats and roses on top of the push pops.

1 HOUR

EASY PEASY

DECOUPAGED INITIALS
by Jennifer Grace

The bride and groom's initials, decoupaged with pretty papers and embellished with ribbons and buttons, make the perfect centrepiece for the top table.

You Will Need

Letter and heart blanks

Patterned papers in two different designs

Lace strips and buttons

Decoupage glue

Varnish

2 HOURS

EASY PEASY

1. Take one of your patterned papers and tear or cut it into little pieces approximately 2cm (¾in) square. Use decoupage glue to adhere the pieces all over the letter and heart blanks, spreading the glue over the top of the paper as well as below, and smoothing out any wrinkles.

2. Take your second patterned paper and tear or cut it into little pieces 2cm (¾in) square. Glue these on top to create bands around the letter and heart shapes.

3. Once you are happy with your design, you need to protect the decorated letters by sealing with a layer of varnish.

4. Embellish the varnished letters using hot glue to attach strips of lace to the paper bands, and then buttons to the lace strips.

WEDDING

POP-UP CAKE CARD
by Marion Elliot

A handmade wedding card is a special reminder of the bridal couple's happy day.
This pretty pop-up cake design would also make a wonderful wedding invitation.

You Will Need

Two sheets of double-sided paper 15cm x 15cm (6in x 6in)

Narrow ribbons

I HOUR

GET STUCK IN

1. Take one piece of paper and fold it in half. Take a second piece of paper and trim it to measure 15cm x 13cm (6in x 5in), then fold it in half too. Cut out a heart shape on the fold of the paper where marked.

2. Now mark the cut lines on the back of the trimmed piece of paper. Starting 5cm (2in) from the top of the paper, draw a 2cm (¾in) long line across the middle of the fold.

3. Draw the remaining lines 2cm (¾in) apart to the following lengths: 4cm (1½in); 6cm (2⅜in); 8cm (3⅛in). Cut along the marked lines using a craft knife and metal ruler. To make the cake layers, push out the paper at each cut, creasing the sides as you go.

4. Trace off the cake plate template and cut out from a contrasting paper.

5. Working on the front of the cake layer paper, stick on the cake plate so that it is parallel to the lowest cake layer. Cut lengths of ribbon to fit across the cake layers and glue in place. Spread a little paper glue onto the back of the narrower cake layer piece of paper and attach it to the front of the wider piece of folded paper, making sure that the cake layers still pop out. Trim the edges of the narrower paper with ribbon.

Full-size templates for this project are available at: www.stitchcraftcreate.co.uk

WEDDING

LOVE HEART NECKLACE
by Dorothy Wood

This elegant necklace would be ideal for the bride's big day featuring silver chain and beautiful Swarovski crystals. You could also make matching earrings to complete the set.

You Will Need

30mm heart metal pearl

Swarovski crystal rainbow beads

Silver eyepins

Silver-plated chain

6mm silver jump rings

Silver bolt ring

Silver headpins

1 HOUR

GET STUCK IN

1. Make 10 crystal bead links: pick up one crystal onto an eyepin, then trim the other end to 7mm (⁹⁄₃₂in); bend the trimmed end over at right angles and use round-nose pliers to form a matching loop.

2. Cut 10 lengths of chain each measuring 2.5cm (1in). Open a loop on a bead link and attach a length.

3. Add another bead link then another length of chain. Repeat to join five lengths of chain and five bead links. Make a second length exactly the same.

4. Make two crystals into dangles. Thread each onto a headpin, trim to 7mm (⁹⁄₃₂in) and make a loop as before.

5. Cut three lengths of chain measuring 5cm (2in). Add one to each bead link. Join the other ends of the prepared chains using a jump ring. Open the jump ring and attach the heart metal pearl then a crystal dangle. Attach a bolt ring using a jump ring to one side. Attach the remaining chain using a jump ring to the other side. Attach a crystal dangle to the end.

WEDDING

WEDDING CARD

by Jane Millard

This lovely wedding card is decorated with a heart and butterfly cut outs, and embellished with rolled flowers.

You Will Need

Single-fold card
13.5cm x 13.5cm
(5¼in x 5¼in)

Cream card

Patterned paper

Green felt

Pearl embellishments

Ribbon

Circle punch

Distress ink pad

1. Cut a piece of cream card measuring 13.3cm x 13.3cm (5⅛in x 5⅛in). Add a square of patterned paper on top leaving a small border all around. Wrap with ribbon and attach to the single-fold card.

2. To make flowers, punch three circles from cream card and cut each into a spiral. Roll up spiral from the outside edge, secure beneath with a little glue, and add a pearl to the centre. Cut two small felt leaves.

3. Use the templates to cut a heart and butterfly from cream card and ink the edges.

4. Attach the heart over the ribbon in the middle of the front of the single-fold card using adhesive foam pads. Add the rolled flowers to the top left-hand side of the heart and stick on the leaves tucked behind. Attach the butterfly shaping the wings and sticking down only the body.

5. Decorate the butterfly body with pearls and add a pearl to top right of the card.

I HOUR

GET STUCK IN

Full-size templates for this project are available at: www.stitchcraftcreate.co.uk

WEDDING

CELEBRATION BUNTING
by Jenny Arnott

Lengths of pretty floral bunting made in a soft green, turquoise and pale pink colour palette are perfect for a summer wedding.

You Will Need

Floral patterned fabrics in several colours and prints

Pink bias binding

I HOUR

GET STUCK IN

1. Use the template to cut your desired number of pennants from your fabrics. Pin each pair of triangles together with right sides facing. Machine stitch down each side of the triangles using a 5mm (³⁄₁₆in) seam allowance and leaving the top edge open.

2. Turn the pennants the right way out. Press, then trim the top edges to neaten. Each pennant should be the same size.

3. Cut a length of bias binding to the desired length. Fold the tape in half lengthways and press to fix crease. Pin the pennants at regular intervals along the binding, leaving a length of at least 50cm (20in) of binding free at each end for hanging.

4. Stitch with matching thread, catching both sides of the binding and the fabric pennants as you sew. To neaten the ends of the binding, fold them over and stitch in place.

Full-size templates for this project are available at: www.stitchcraftcreate.co.uk

WEDDING

TISSUE PAPER FLOWERS
by Jennifer Grace

These tissue paper flowers with their beaded centres will add a special touch to wedding table decorations and can be made to match your colour theme.

You Will Need

Tissue paper

Silver wire

Seed beads

30 MINUTES

EASY PEASY

1. Cut 10 rectangles of tissue paper measuring 12cm x 18cm (4¾in x 7in). Lay the paper rectangles on top of each other to make a neat stack. Making sure a short edge is nearest to you, begin to concertina fold – fan style – making the folds approximately 1cm (⅜in) apart.

2. Cut a 5cm (2in) length of wire and twist it tightly around the middle

of the tissue paper fan, folding the excess flat against the back of the flower. Cut the ends of the flattened fan into arch shapes. Unfold the flower to reveal the scalloped petals.

3. Gently lift the tissue paper layers to separate them, to give the flower some dimension, and pull them lightly to join the petal gaps (there is no need to glue them together).

4. Put a 2.5cm (1in) dollop of tacky glue into the flower centre and sprinkle on some seed beads. Leave to dry.

5. Cut two tissue paper leaves freehand, approximately 8cm (3⅛in) long, and stick to the underside of the flower to hide the wire.

SHAPED PLACE CARDS
by Marion Elliot

These place cards are the ideal way to help wedding guests to find their seat at the reception – you could also adapt the designs to suit your theme.

You Will Need

Patterned paper pack

White card

1 HOUR

EASY PEASY

1. Trace off the house, bird and cake templates and cut out from thin white card.

2. Score along the fold lines where marked, and fold up the base of each place setting.

3. Trace off all the bird, house and cake details and cut out from patterned papers.

4. Stick the patterned paper details in place on the front of the place settings. To complete, simply write a guest's name on each place setting.

5. For a stylish and sophisticated alternative to funky patterned papers, you could decide instead to use plain papers adding flashes of silver and gold metallic papers for the detailing.

Full-size templates for this project are available at: www.stitchcraftcreate.co.uk

WEDDING

RING CUSHION
by Louise Butt

A ring cushion is a lovely way to present the rings at the wedding ceremony and this one is the perfect size for a little pageboy to carry down the aisle.

You Will Need

3.25mm (US size 3) knitting needles

4mm (US size 6) knitting needles

1 x 50g ball Patons Fairytale 4 Ply in following colours: snow white and blue

3.5mm (US size E/4) crochet hook

Toy filling

1 DAY

GET STUCK IN

1. Knit the ring cushion following the pattern below:

Back
Using 3.25mm needles and white yarn, cast on 32sts.
Work stocking stitch for 14cm (5½in).
Cast off.

Front
Using 3.25mm needles and white yarn, cast on 32sts.
P 1 row.
Row 1: *cross 2 R, k4, rep from * to last 2sts, cross 2 R.
Row 2 and all even numbered rows: P.
Row 3: K1, *cross 2 L as follows miss next stitch, knit into back of

2nd st, then knit into back of both sts, slip off needle together, k2, cross 2 R, rep from * to last st, k1.

Row 5: K2, *cross 2 L, cross 2 R, K2, rep from * to end.

Row 7: K2, *k1, cross 2 R, k3, rep from * to end.

Row 9: K2, *cross 2 R, cross 2 L, k2, rep from * to end.

Row 11: K1, *cross 2 R, k2, cross 2 L, rep from * to last st, k1.

Row 12: P

Rep rows 1–12, until knitting measures 14cm (5½in).

Cast off.

Border

Using 3.25mm needles and blue yarn, cast on 3sts.

Row 1: K.

Row 2: P.

Row 3: K1, m1, k to end.

Row 4: P.

Row 5: K1, m1, yon, K2tog, k to end

Row 6: P.

Row 7: Sl1, k1, psso, k to end.

Row 8: P.

Row 9: Sl1, k1, psso, k to end.

Row 10: P.

Rep from row 3 until border measures 14cm (5½in) – 5 points.

K

P

K

P

Rep from row 3 three times. Cast off.

2. To make up the ring cushion, place the front and back together with right sides facing and with the border sandwiched in between. Sew through all three pieces of knitting to join leaving a 5cm (2in) gap for turning. Turn right side out and stuff with toy filling. Sew gap closed.

3. To make the ties, using a 3.5mm crochet hook and white yarn, crochet two 25cm (10in) chains. Attach these to the top right of the cushion with a couple of small neat hand stitches.

CONE BASKET FAVOURS
by Marion Elliot

These little cone baskets will look lovely on a wedding table filled with sweets.
They are quick and easy to make taking just half an hour each.

You Will Need

Double-sided paper pack
30cm x 30cm (12in x 12in)

Lace edge paper punch

Organza ribbon

Thin card

30 MINUTES

EASY PEASY

1. Trace off the cone template and cut out from thin card to make a template. Draw around the template onto double-sided paper and cut out. To make the cone, curve the sides of the paper around, using double-sided tape to stick the edges together.

2. Take a sheet of contrasting paper and punch a decorative border along one edge.

3. Trim off the punched edge to give you a strip of paper lace approximately 15cm (6in) wide. Cut lengths of the paper lace strip and use to hide the paper join on the cone and to decorate around the rim.

4. Cut two slits on either side of the cone, directly opposite each other. Thread the ends of a length of organza ribbon through the slits and tie the ends to make a hanging loop.

Full-size templates for this project are available at: www.stitchcraftcreate.co.uk

WEDDING

FLOWER FASCINATOR
by Carol May

This accessory can be stitched onto a headband or onto a hair clip.
Alternatively, attach a safety pin for an impressive wedding corsage.

You Will Need

Black, red and white patterned ribbons

Large white button and small pink flower-shaped button

Red sewing thread

Headband

1 HOUR

EASY PEASY

1. Take the black patterned ribbon and fold and pleat the ribbon petals one at a time, hand stitching as you go. Make five petals in a circle.

2. Take the red patterned ribbon and fold and pleat this on top of the first circle of ribbon petals, again making five petals in a circle.

3. Take thin white patterned ribbon and stitch a group of loops over the second circle of ribbon loops. You can cut the folds or leave uncut as you prefer.

4. Place the small button on top of the large button and sew in the centre of the ribbon flower. Sew the flower securely to the headband.

WEDDING

NEW BABY

BABY'S ONESIE COOKIES
by Fiona Pearce

To celebrate baby's arrival bake up a batch of cookies shaped as little baby bodysuits. You could also make these adorable cookies in pink for a baby girl.

You Will Need

Batch of cookie dough

White royal icing

Blue or pink food colourings

Disposable piping bags

No. 2 piping nozzle

Squeeze bottles

---

1 HOUR

EASY PEASY

1. Roll out the cookie dough to 5mm (³⁄₁₆in) and use a small knife to cut out the cookies into the bodysuit shape using the onesie template as a guide. Bake according to your recipe, then leave to cool completely before decorating.

2. Equally divide the royal icing into two bowls. Leaving one half white, colour the other half with blue or pink food colouring.

3. Using half of each batch of royal icing, fill disposable piping bags fitted with no. 2 piping nozzle. Add a few drops of water to the remaining royal icing and mix until a runny consistency is achieved. Fill squeeze bottles with the runny royal icing. Pipe royal icing from the piping bag around the edge of each cookie. Fill the piped outline with the runny royal icing from the squeeze bottle, using a cocktail stick to guide the icing into empty spaces or to pop any air bubbles.

4. Once each cookie is filled, squeeze little dots of another colour of the runny royal icing onto the wet icing to achieve the polka dot effect.

5. Leave the cookies to dry for 3–4 hours before piping the garment details on the top of the cookies.

Full-size templates for this project are available at: www.stitchcraftcreate.co.uk

NEW BABY

HAT AND MITTEN SET
by Louise Butt

This lovely set would make the perfect gift for parents of a new baby, but as several sizes are given you could make it for a first Christmas or birthday gift too.

You Will Need

Set 3.25mm (US size 3) double-pointed needles

2 x 50g ball Patons Fairytale 4 Ply shade 04381

Stitch marker

Tapestry needle

1 DAY

GET STUCK IN

1. Choose the size of hat you would like to knit and follow the pattern below. Note the pattern has been given for four sizes to fit head circumferences as follows: newborn 30cm (12in); 6-month-old 35.5cm (14in); 12-month-old 40.5cm (16in); 12–24-month-old 46cm (18in). Cast on 90 (96, 108, 120) sts and arrange sts over 4 needles taking care not to twist the stitches, and placing a marker to show beginning and end of round. Work a k1, p1 rib for 10 rounds. K 5 rounds.

Bobble round 1: *K5, make bobble (MB) as follows (yon, k1) three times in next st; turn sl1, P5; turn sl1, k5; turn p2tog 3 times; turn sl1, k2tog, psso, rep from * to end of round.
Next round: *K5, k1tbl, rep from * to end of round.
K5 rounds.
Bobble round 2: K3, *(yon, k1) three times in next st; turn sl1, p5; turn sl1, k5; turn p2tog 3 times; turn sl1, k2tog, psso, k5, rep from * to last 3sts, *(yon, k1) three times in next st; turn sl1, p5; turn sl1, k5; turn p2tog

3 times; turn sl1, k2tog, psso, k2.
Next round: *K5, k1tbl, rep from * to end of round.
Knit every round until knitting measures: 12.5cm (14cm, 16.5cm, 18cm) [5in (5½in, 6½in, 7in)]
Next row: *K4, k2tog, rep from * to end. 75 (80, 90, 100) sts
Next row: K.
Next row: *K3, k2tog, rep from * to end. 60 (64, 72, 80) sts
Next row: K.
Next row: *K2, k2tog, rep from * to end. 45 (48, 54, 60) sts
Next row: K.
Next row: *K1, k2tog, rep from * to end. 30 (32, 36, 40) sts
Next row: K.
Next row: K2tog to end. 15 (16, 18, 20) sts
Next row: K.
Next row: K1 (0, 0, 0), k2tog to end. 8 (8, 9, 10) sts
Cut yarn, thread onto a tapestry needle and draw through sts, then fasten on reverse of hat. Sew in loose ends on wrong side of fabric.

2. Knit the mittens following the pattern below. Make 2.
Cast on 24 (28, 36, 44) sts and arrange sts over 4 needles taking care not to twist the stitches, and placing a marker to show beginning and end of round.

Work k1, p1 rib until knitting measures 4cm (4cm, 5cm, 5cm) [1½in (1½in, 2in, 2in)].
Increase round: *K6 (7, 9, 11), m1, rep from * to end of round. 28 (32, 40, 48) sts
Next round: K
Increase round: *K7 (8, 10, 12), m1, rep from * to end of round. 32 (36, 44, 52) sts
Next row: MB, *k4 (5, 7, 9) MB, rep from * once more, k to end of round.
K every round until knitting measures 9cm (9cm, 11cm, 13cm) [3½in (3½in, 4½in, 5in)].
Next round: *K2, k2tog, rep from * to end of round. 24 (27, 33, 39) sts
Next round: K.
Next round: *K1, k2tog, rep from * to end of round. 16 (18, 22, 26) sts

Next round: *K2tog to end of round. 8 (9, 11, 13) sts
Next round: K0 (1, 1, 1), *k2tog, rep from * to end of round. 4 (5, 6, 7) sts
Cut yarn and thread through sts, pull tightly and fasten off on the wrong side.

BUTTERFLY BUNTING
by Claire Garland

This fun cuddly bunting felted with butterflies and pompoms in soft vintage colours is perfect for decorating a new baby's nursery.

You Will Need

Set 5mm (US size 8) double-pointed needles

1 x 100g ball of M S Roving Wool in following colours: blue, pink, lilac and cream

White, pink and grey felt

Embroidery thread

Pompom making set

2 HOURS

GET STUCK IN

1. Knit the bunting pennants following the pattern below: Cast on 30sts onto one needle as follows:
Step 1: Hold needle with stitches in left hand.
Step 2: Hold 2 empty dpns parallel in right hand.
Step 3: Slip 1st cast on st purlwise onto the dpn closest to you and off the needle in the left hand, then slip the next cast on st onto the dpn furthest away and off the RH needle. Repeat step 3 until all 30sts are divided onto the 2 parallel dpns, 15sts on the front dpn and 15sts on the back
Slide sts to the other ends of the

dpns, working yarn at back. RS facing, cont working in the rnd, beg by knitting the sts on the back dpn – work sts over 2 dpns, using a 3rd dpn to knit with.

Rnd 1: K30. Place marker.

Rnd 2: (dec) K1, sl1, kl, psso, k9, k2tog, k1, k1, sl1, kl, psso, k9, k2tog, k1. 26sts (13 sts on each needle)

Rnds 3, 5, 7, 9, 11, 13, 15: K.

Rnd 4: (dec) K1, sl1, kl, psso, k7, k2tog, k1, k1, sl1, kl, psso, k7, k2tog, k1. 22sts

Rnd 6: (dec) K1, sl1, kl, psso, k5, k2tog, k1, k1, sl1, kl, psso, k5, k2tog, k1. 18sts

Rnd 8: (dec) K1, sl1, kl, psso, k3, k2tog, k1, k1, sl1, kl, psso, k3, k2tog, k1. 14sts

Rnd 10: (dec) K1, sl1, kl, psso, k1, k2tog, k1, k1, sl1, kl, psso, k1, k2tog, k1. 10sts

Rnd 12: (dec) K2, sl1, kl, psso, k1, k2, sl1, kl, psso, k1. 8sts

Rnd 14: (dec) [Sl1, kl, psso, k2tog] twice. 4sts

Rnd 16: (dec) Sl1, kl, psso, k2tog. 2sts

Cut yarn, thread end through rem 2sts, pull up tight and secure end.

2. To felt the pennants, soak in reasonably hot water, then rub in a little hand soap. Wash out the soap then squeeze out the water. Rub each pennant in between your hands: as you do this the yarn will matt together to give you the felted look you are after – if the pennant is still very damp, rub it in between a tea towel. Keep checking the pennant for shape and re-moulding if necessary. Continue rubbing and agitating until the pennant is quite dry and well felted, re-shaping one last time before placing on a radiator to dry.

3. Make a pompom from coloured yarn to finish each pennant. Make a medium-sized pompom and sew to the base of the pennant (opposite the cast on edge).

4. Use the template to cut butterflies from the felt, one for each pennant. To sew the butterflies onto each pennant, work straight stitches through the middle of the butterfly to make the body, then stitch two long stitches onto the knitted fabric for the antennae.

5. To join the pennants simply thread the desired length of yarn through the cast on edge of each pennant leaving enough yarn at each end for hanging.

Full-size templates for this project are available at: www.stitchcraftcreate.co.uk

NEW BABY

FLOWER CUPCAKES
by Kate Kerly

Pretty cupcakes decorated with swirls of buttercream and topped with delicate flowers and edible glitter make a great treat for the welcome baby party.

You Will Need

Batch of 12 cupcakes

White sugarpaste

Pink and blue food colouring

White sugar pearls

Buttercream

Edible silver glitter

Patterned scroll roller

Flower cutter

Disposable piping bag

Star piping nozzle

30 MINUTES

EASY PEASY

1. Take some of the white sugarpaste and colour it blue or pink with a few drops of food colouring. Roll out the coloured paste to 5mm (³⁄₁₆in) thick. Roll the scroll roller over the sugarpaste to indent the pattern, and use the flower cutter to cut out 12 flowers. Set aside to harden.

2. Once the flowers have dried completely, add white sugar pearls to the centres using a dot of buttercream, then leave to dry. Fill a piping bag fitted with a large star nozzle with buttercream. Pipe large swirls on top of each cupcake. Place a flower on top of the buttercream.

3. To finish the cupcakes dust each one with edible silver glitter and dot a few of the white sugar pearls around the edges.

NEW BABY

RIBBON MEMORY BOARD
by Linda Clements

This notice board is perfect to display photos and mementoes of a baby's first year. The size can be increased by starting with larger squares.

You Will Need

Fat quarter print fabric and 0.5m (½yd) plain fabric

Wadding (batting) 38cm (15in) square

Corkboard 38cm (15in) square

6m (6½yd) of 1.3cm (½in) wide ribbon and 2m (2yd) white ric rac

Dark orange stranded cotton (floss)

12 buttons

Card 38cm (15in) square

Hot glue gun

1. Cut 16 10.2cm (4in) squares from plain fabric and nine from print fabric. Arrange alternately, with one square in the first row, three in the second row, then five, seven, five, three and one.

2. Sew the squares in each row together using 6mm (¼in) seams and press. Sew the rows to each other and press. Trim off the triangles to make the patchwork square but don't cut up to the points – leave 6mm (¼in).

3. Cut two fabric strips 5cm x 38cm (2in x 15in) and two 5cm x 46cm (2in x 18in). Sew the shorter strips to the sides and longer strips to top and bottom. Press seams.

4. Pin the wadding on the back and quilt using the piglet template. Cut strips of ribbon to go across the diagonal lines of the patchwork and overlap to the back. Pin in place, keeping the ribbon taut, and sew through at the intersections. Press and sew buttons at the intersections.

5. Put the patchwork on the corkboard and use a hot glue gun to glue in place at the back, keeping the work straight. Glue ric rac around the edge. Glue a ribbon hanging loop at the back and a sheet of card over the back to finish neatly.

1 DAY

GET STUCK IN

Full-size templates for this project are available at: www.stitchcraftcreate.co.uk

NEW BABY

ELEPHANT CUSHION

by Mary Fogg

This lovely cushion with its sweet elephant appliqué design
would make a lovely new baby gift to decorate the nursery.

You Will Need

Fabric for cushion front:
28.5cm x 41.5cm
(11¼in x 16¼in)

Fabric for cushion back:
28.5cm x 41.5cm
(11¼in x 16¼in)

Fabric for appliqué:
14cm x 21cm (5½in x 8¼in)

Red and blue felt
for appliqué

Fusible webbing

Black and white
sewing thread

Toy filling

1. Iron the fusible webbing to
the appliqué fabric (if you have some
spare you could use the same fabric
as the cushion backing) following
the manufacturer's instructions.
Use the template reversed to
cut out the elephant body and
tail from the appliqué fabric and
fix to the middle of the cushion
front, making sure the design is
the correct way round. Using the
machine zigzag stitch, sew all the
way around the appliqué design.

2. Use the template to cut
out the eye and ear from red felt
and the water spray from blue felt.
Use a straight stitch to attach,
and work a large cross stitch in
the centre of the elephant's eye.

3. Place the cushion front and
back right sides together, and pin.
Machine stitch around the edges
using a 1.5cm (⅝in) seam allowance
and leaving a gap for turning.

4. Trim the corners; turn
the cushion cover through to
the right side. Press gently and
stuff so the toy filling reaches
into the corners. Slip stitch the
opening closed by hand.

2 HOURS

GET STUCK IN

Full-size templates for this project are available at: www.stitchcraftcreate.co.uk

NEW BABY

'A STAR IS BORN' CARD

by Jane Millard

To celebrate a new little star in the world, make this stunning card using a star die cut. Make the design using pink paper and felt for a baby girl.

You Will Need

White single-fold card 13.5cm x 13.5cm (5¼in x 5¼in)

Patterned paper

Textured white card

Pink or blue button

Pink or blue felt

Adhesive pearl

Small and large star die cuts

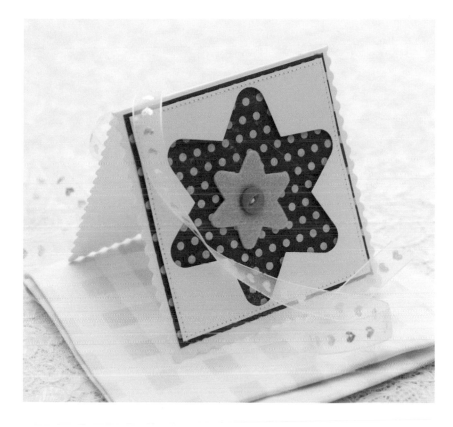

1. Cut a piece of blue or pink patterned paper measuring 13cm x 13cm (5in x 5in). Attach to the front of the single-fold card.

2. Cut a piece of textured white card measuring 12cm x 12cm (4¾in x 4¾in) and die cut a large star in its centre. Machine stitch all around the edges and use adhesive foam pads to attach it to the front of the card.

3. Die cut a small star from the felt and add the button on top. Use an adhesive foam pad to secure inside the centre of the large die cut star shape. Stick on the adhesive pearl in the top left corner of the card to finish.

1 HOUR

GET STUCK IN

LITTLE FELT STORKS

by Zoe Larkins

These cute little stuffed hanging storks make an excellent gift for the expectant mother or can be used as gift tags on presents for the new baby.

You Will Need

White, pink, yellow and blue felt

Toy filling

Wide yellow and narrow patterned ribbons

Black crystal bead

1 HOUR

EASY PEASY

1. Use the templates to cut out two stork shapes from white felt, one beak and two feet from yellow felt, and one bundle of joy from blue or pink felt. Set aside one of the stork shapes.

2. Using the photograph as your guide, pin the beak and bundle of joy onto the second stork shape and stitch in place. Sew on a black crystal bead eye.

3. Pin the embellished stork, right side uppermost, to the set aside stork shape. Sandwiched between them, place a ribbon loop for hanging at the top and two lengths of yellow ribbon at the base for legs. Sew the feet to the end of the ribbon legs.

4. Sew all the way around the stork's body, adding the toy stuffing before finishing the stitching.

5. Add a little patterned ribbon bow to the stork's neck and use black thread to embroider a few long stitches onto the wing for definition.

Full-size templates for this project are available at: www.stitchcraftcreate.co.uk

NEW BABY

WASHING LINE CARD
by Debbie Pyne

Nothing says a new baby has arrived better than a line full of
tiny clothes – stitch up yours from cute fabric scraps.

You Will Need

Cream single-fold
card size DL

Pink and yellow felt

Scraps of patterned fabric

30 MINUTES ⏰

EASY PEASY 🎁

1. Use the templates to cut out two bibs, two onesies and two little pairs of socks from the felt and fabric scraps. Sew a running stitch border all the way around the baby clothes.

2. Orientate the single-fold card so the fold is at the top and arrange the baby clothes on the front of the card. Draw on the washing line and poles, first in pencil, then in a colour pen of your choice.

3. Glue the washing onto the card with fabric glue. For the pegs, cut small rectangles of felt and glue to overlap the washing line and the clothes.

Full-size templates for this project are available at: www.stitchcraftcreate.co.uk

NEW BABY

HALLOWEEN

SPOOKY EYEBALLS
by Claire Garland

You can have so much fun with these knitted eyeballs – they are perfect
for slipping into a 'trick or treat' bag for a scary surprise.

You will need

Set 3.5mm (US size 4)
double-pointed needles

1 x 25g ball Patons Fab
DK acrylic yarn cream

Toy filling

Red sewing thread

1.8cm (¾in) diameter toy
eye with plastic washer

2 HOURS

GET STUCK IN

1. Knit the eyeball following
the pattern below:

Cast on 6sts.
Rnd 1: K6.
Work as i-cord as follows:
Slide sts to other end of needle
without turning. Keeping gauge
tight, pull working yarn across
the back of the i-cord.
Rnd 2: (inc) [Kf&b] 6 times. 12sts
Rnd 3: Divide 12sts evenly over 3
dpns, 4sts on each needle. K.
With righ side facing and keeping the
gauge fairly tight on the first round,

work in the round as follows:
Rnd 4: (inc) [K1, kf&b] 6 times.
18sts
Rnds 5, 7, 9, 11: K.
Rnd 6: (inc) [K2, kf&b] 6 times.
24sts
Rnd 8: (inc) [K3, kf&b] 6 times.
30sts
Rnd 10: (inc) [K4, kf&b] 6 times.
36sts
Rnd 12: (dec) [K4, k2tog] 6 times.
30sts
Rnds 13, 15, 17, 19: K.
Rnd 14: (dec) [K3, k2tog] 6 times.
24sts

Rnd 16: (dec) [K2, k2tog]
6 times. 18sts
Rnd 18: (dec) [K1, k2tog] 6
times. 12sts
Fit in the toy eye and stuff
with the toy filling.
Rnd 20: (dec) [K2tog] 6 times. 6sts
Cut yarn, thread end through the
remaining 6sts, pull up tight and
secure the end.

2. Sew a few lines through
the yarn with the red thread to
create the bloodshot effect.

PUMPKIN PINCUSHION
by Sue Trevor

This Jack o' lantern pincushion is perfect for all those autumn season's sewing sessions. It can also be used as a decoration for a Halloween party.

You Will Need

Orange, green and black felt

One skein orange stranded cotton (floss)

Orange and green sewing threads

Toy filling

2 HOURS

GET STUCK IN

1. Cut a 20cm (8in) diameter circle from the orange felt. From the green felt cut the following: one piece 12cm x 3cm (4¾in x 1⅛in), two pieces 12cm x 5mm (4¾in x 3/16in) and a star shape. Use the templates to cut the eyes, nose and mouth from the black felt.

2. Using the orange sewing thread, stitch a line of running stitches approximately 3mm (⅛in) from the outer edge of the orange felt circle all the way around.

3. Pull the stitches tightly to gather the circle into a ball and stuff firmly with toy filling. Sew up the top. To create the pumpkin segments, thread a needle with the unstranded orange skein and working from the top of the pumpkin, stitch through to the bottom and round to the top again, 12 times in all and tying a knot to finish.

4. To make the pumpkin stem, roll up the larger piece of green felt, tacking (basting) as you go.

5. Stitch the stem to the star shaped piece. Take the long thin pieces of green felt and blanket stitch down one side, pulling each stitch tightly as you go to make the strips coil up to make the tendrils. Stitch the tendrils in place at the top of the pumpkin, then stitch the stalk on top.

6. Glue or stitch the eyes, nose and mouth to the front of the pumpkin to finish.

Full-size templates for this project are available at: www.stitchcraftcreate.co.uk

HALLOWEEN

GHOSTLY CUPCAKES
by Fiona Pearce

It's truly scary just how delicious these miniature ghost cupcakes taste – your Halloween guests are sure to ask for more.

You Will Need

One batch of mini cupcakes baked in white cases

White sugarpaste

Black royal icing

Buttercream

Marshmallows

Disposable piping bag

No. 2 piping nozzle

1 HOUR

EASY PEASY

1. Cover the top of each cupcake with a thin layer of buttercream. Stack two marshmallows on top of the centre of each cupcake, using buttercream to stick them together. Add a little bit of buttercream on the top marshmallow to hold the sugarpaste covering in place.

2. Use a non-stick rolling pin to roll out some of the white sugarpaste in a rough circle shape approximately 3mm (⅛in) thick and about four times the cupcake diameter. Gently drape the sugarpaste over the top of the marshmallows to cover the whole cupcake and case.

3. Use a small knife to trim away any excess sugarpaste from around the base of the cupcake. Fill a piping bag fitted with the no. 2 piping nozzle with black royal icing and use to pipe eyes and a mouth onto each ghost. Allow the royal icing to dry before serving.

HALLOWEEN

HALLOWEEN TREAT BAG
by Jane Millard

Give the kids a treat with a special Halloween sweet bag decorated with scary monster embellishment.

You Will Need

Black and orange card

Cellophane bags size C6

Monster sticker

Black gingham ribbon

Star border punch

30 MINUTES

EASY PEASY

1. Cut a piece of black card measuring 12cm x 12.5cm (4¾in x 4⅞in). Punch one of the shorter edges with the star border punch, then fold in half.

2. Cut a piece of orange card measuring 11.5cm x 4cm (4½in x 1½in) and attach to the folded black card just above the punched border.

3. Fill a cellophane bag with treats and seal. Stick the folded black card over the top of the bag. Decorate with a bow tied from the black gingham ribbon and add the monster sticker. Add three punched stars to the bottom right-hand corner of the orange panel.

HALLOWEEN

HARVEST COASTERS
by Linda Clements

These coasters, made in warm shades and decorated with easy blanket stitch appliqué, will suit most kitchen styles and make useful Thanksgiving gifts.

You Will Need:

Outer background fabric: Two 16.5cm (6½in) squares per coaster

Inner background fabric: One 11.4cm (4½in) square per coaster

Yellow print for pear appliqué or green print for apple appliqué

Scraps of green fabrics for leaf and stalk appliqués

Fusible webbing

Wadding (batting)

Dark brown stranded cotton (floss)

1. Back the inner background fabric square with fusible webbing. Use the template to cut out the small hexagon from the web-backed fabric. Fuse the hexagon in the centre of an outer background square.

2. Cut a 7.6cm (3in) square of green or yellow print for the apple or pear. Cut a 5cm (2in) square each of green fabric and dark green for leaf and stalk.

3. Back the appliqué fabric squares with fusible webbing. Cut out the shapes. Peel off the papers and position the fruit, leaf and stalk on the hexagon; fuse into place. Use three strands of embroidery thread to blanket stitch around the appliqués and the inner hexagon.

4. Shape the background squares to the coaster shape using the large hexagon template.

5. Cut wadding 6mm (¼in) smaller and pin to the back of the fronts. Pin fronts and backs together; sew 6mm (¼in) seam leaving a turning gap. Turn; press in open edges; topstitch close to edge.

6 HOURS
GET STUCK IN

Full-size templates for this project are available at: www.stitchcraftcreate.co.uk

HALLOWEEN

GHOULISH GARLAND
by Ali Burdon

This simple garland decorated with hand-sewn felt ghouls and skulls will add a shiver to your Halloween celebrations.

You Will Need

Black and white felt

Black and white stranded cotton (floss)

Black gingham ribbon

Toy filling

3 HOURS

GET STUCK IN

1. Use the templates to draw a skull and ghost onto cardboard and cut out. Use the card templates to cut out 12 skulls and 10 ghosts from white felt.

2. From black felt cut 11 pairs of eyes (circles). Also cut out five small jellybean shapes for the ghosts' mouths. Using three strands of black thread, sew on the eyes and embroider teeth onto the six skulls.

3. Sew the eyes and mouths onto five of the ghosts. Place a ghost front and back together with the front piece on top and facing up. Sew together around the edges using three strands of white thread and running stitch, stopping 2cm (¾in) from your start point to pad the shape with toy filling using a pencil or crochet hook to push the stuffing into place. Complete stitching and fasten off. Repeat to make all the skulls and all the ghosts.

4. Turn under 5cm (2in) at either end of a length of black gingham ribbon to create hanging loops. Firmly stitch the ghosts and skulls at evenly spaced intervals (around 12cm/4¾in apart) along the ribbon.

Full-size templates for this project are available at: www.stitchcraftcreate.co.uk

HALLOWEEN

PUMPKIN CUPCAKES
by Ruth Clemens

This spooky collection of pumpkin cupcakes is sure to impress your guests this Halloween. Experiment with black sugarpaste bats and piped cobwebs for a fun variation.

You Will Need

One batch cupcakes baked in orange and black cases

White sugarpaste

White sugar florist paste (SFP)

Black, orange and green gel paste colours

Buttercream

Royal icing

Fluted circle cutter 5.5cm (2¼in) diameter and ivy leaf cutter

Large open star piping nozzle

Disposable piping bag

1. Knead together equal amounts of white sugarpaste and SFP, and colour portions orange, green and black. Roll out black and orange pastes to 2mm (³⁄₃₂in) thick. Cut out three fluted circles from each colour and set aside to dry.

2. Make three pumpkins: roll a 2.5cm (1in) orange paste ball; flatten the base slightly. Use a cocktail stick to mark vertical lines on the sides.

3. Cut out three leaves from thinly rolled out green paste. Secure to the pumpkin tops with a dab of water. Make a hole in the top of the pumpkin through the leaf to insert the stalk rolled from a tiny green paste sausage with tapered end.

4. Secure each pumpkin to a black disc. Cut tendrils from long thin green paste strips wound around a cocktail stick and attach.

5. Fill a piping bag fitted with an large open star nozzle with buttercream and pipe swirls onto each cupcake. Place the cupcake toppers in position on top.

30 MINUTES

EASY PEASY

HALLOWEEN

HALLOWEEN CARD

by Jayne Schofield

Cross stitch this Halloween design for a spooky party invite. The black and orange really stand out well on the green greeting card base.

You Will Need

Black 14-count aida

Orange, rust, white, purple, lilac, yellow and black stranded cotton (floss): DMC colours 402, 3776, blanc, 155, 341, 725 and 310

Green single-fold card size A6

1 DAY

GET STUCK IN

1. Cross stitch the design onto aida with stranded cotton following the chart in the Charts section. Use two strands of stranded cotton throughout. Trim your embroidery as marked on the chart.

2. Fray back one row of aida all the way around the finished stitched piece to give a soft edge.

3. Place strips of double-sided tape on the back of your embroidery and attach it to the front of the single-fold card making sure it is central. Stick down firmly.

HALLOWEEN

PUMPKIN BROOCHES
By Sue Burley

These pumpkin brooches make the ideal addition to any Halloween outfit. Alternatively, they could be attached to a hair clip or a headband if you prefer.

You Will Need

Orange and black felt

Black stranded cotton (floss)

Black buttons

Toy filling

Brooch pins

1 HOUR

EASY PEASY

1. Use the templates to cut out two pumpkins from the orange felt for each pumpkin and your choice of mouth, and eyes and nose from black felt. (If you prefer you could use two black buttons for the eyes.)

2. Using two strands of the embroidery thread, sew or glue the eyes, nose and mouth onto one of the pumpkin pieces.

3. Place the two pumpkin pieces together with the front facing up, and sew together around the edges with blanket stitch, leaving a small gap for stuffing.

4. Use the toy filling to stuff your pumpkins. When they are as plump as you want, sew the gap closed. Sew the brooch pins onto the back of the pumpkins to finish.

Full-size templates for this project are available at: www.stitchcraftcreate.co.uk

HALLOWEEN

MONSTER GOODIES BOX

by Jane Millard

This treat box made from punched black card and tissue paper is a perfect alternative to a party bag for a Halloween gathering.

You Will Need

Black card size A4 (US letter)

Purple tissue paper

Halloween stickers

Black ribbon

Orange ric rac

Star border punch

1 HOUR

GET STUCK IN

1. Cut a wide strip along the length of the black A4 card measuring 18cm (7in) wide. Score at 7cm (2¾in) lengthwise and every 7cm (2¾in) along the width, leaving a 2cm (¾in) tab. Along the bottom edge of the card, cut into shorter score lines, cutting off short tab. Use the star border punch to punch a decorative border along the top edge of the card.

2. Cut a piece of purple tissue paper measuring 40cm x 31cm (15⅝in x 12⅜in) and fold it in half. Use double-sided tape to stick the folded edge of the tissue paper inside the box under the punched line, and trim the unfolded edge with pinking shears. Assemble the box folding the 2cm (¾in) tab inside the box and sticking the bottom flaps down with glue.

3. Fill the box with your treats then tie the tissue paper with lengths of ribbon and ric rac. Attach a ric rac border around the box beneath the punched border and decorate with Halloween stickers.

PUMPKIN TEA COSY
by Claire Garland

This spooky pumpkin tea cosy is perfect for a
Halloween tea-time surprise – children will love it.

You Will Need

5mm (US size 8)
knitting needles

1 x 100g ball Rowan
Creative Focus Worsted
in following colours:
orange (A) and green (B)

White and brown yarn

2 DAYS

FANCY A
CHALLENGE

1. Knit the tea cosy
following the pattern below:

Sides (make 2)
Cast on 40 sts.
Row 1 (RS): Using A,
[K6, p2] 5 times.
Row 2 Using A, [k2, p6] 5 times.
Rows 1 and 2 form patt.
Cont in patt (Row 2) until side
measures 15cm (6in), ending WS.

Shape top
Keeping patt correct, cont as follows:
Next row (RS): (dec) K6, p2tog,
rep from * to end. 35sts
Next row: *K1, p6, rep
from * to end.
Next row: (dec) K5, p2tog,
rep from * to end. 30sts
Next row: (dec) P4, k2tog,
rep from * to end. 25sts
Next row: (dec) K3, p2tog,
rep from * to end. 20sts
Next row: (dec) P2, k2tog,
rep from * to end. 15sts

Stalk
Change to yarn B.
Next row: *K1, p1, rep

from * to last stitch, k1.
Next row: *P1, k1, rep
from * to last stitch, p1.
Rep last 2 rows twice.
Next row: (dec) *K1, p2tog,
rep from * to end. 10sts
Next row: *K1, p1, rep
from * to end.
Next row: (dec) K2tog 5 times. 5sts.
Cast off.

2. Join sides leaving spout and
handle openings. Embroider face
using the photograph as a guide.

SCARY COOKIE LOLLIES
by Ruth Clemens

These fun shaped cookies on a stick will be irresistible for any little monster at your Halloween party celebrations.

You Will Need

Six Halloween-shaped cookies baked on lolly sticks

White sugarpaste

Black, orange and green gel paste colours

Royal icing

Bat, ghost and pumpkin cookie cutters

Disposable piping bags

No. 2 piping nozzles

White disc sprinkles

1. Divide the white sugarpaste into thirds and colour two of the portions orange and black. Roll out each sugarpaste portion to 3mm (⅛in) thick and cut out using the corresponding cookie cutter (see photograph).

2. Use the cut out sugarpaste shapes to cover the relevant cookies and secure using a light brush of water.

3. Colour portions of the royal icing green, orange and black, keeping one portion white. Fill piping bags fitted with the no. 2 nozzles and pipe the outlines of the cookies using the corresponding colour.

4. Now add the fine detail. For the pumpkin cookies, pipe lines of orange to define the pumpkin's shape, then add a leafy top using the green royal icing. For the bat cookies, pipe on two small bulbs in black for the eyes. For the ghost cookies, pipe two small bulbs of royal icing to secure the two white disc sprinkle eyes, then pipe small bulbs of black for the pupils.

1 HOUR

EASY PEASY

'TRICK OR TREAT' BAGS

by Linda Clements

These fun bags are perfect for collecting treats on Halloween.
The materials list and instructions are to make one bag.

You Will Need:

Print 1: Five 7.6cm (3in) squares for bag front, 20.3cm (8in) square for bag back and four strips 5cm x 35.5cm (2in x 14in) for handles

Print 2: Four 7.6cm (3in) squares

Black fabric: 30.5cm (12in) square and 20.3cm x 39.4cm (8in x 15½in) for lining

Scraps of fabric

Fusible webbing

White and black stranded cotton (floss)

1. Sew the nine 7.6cm (3in) squares together in three rows of three, in alternate colours, using 6mm (¼in) seams. Press seams.

2. Back the black fabric square with fusible webbing (enough for three motifs). Use the templates and follow the instructions given for fusing and embroidery.

3. Place bag front and back right sides facing and sew along bottom.

4. For the handles, sew two strips right sides together down the long sides. Turn right way; press. Repeat with other strips. Lay the lining fabric right side up. Pin handles in position at short ends, facing *inwards*. Put the bag front on top, right side down. Pin together, aligning edges and sew together all round, leaving a gap in one long side. Remove pins, clip corners, turn right side out. Press gap edges under.

5. Quilt if desired. Fold the bag in half and machine sew down the sides 3mm (⅛in) from the edge. Blanket stitch down the sides with six strands of black stranded cotton.

4 HOURS

GET STUCK IN

Full-size templates for this project are available at: www.stitchcraftcreate.co.uk

HALLOWEEN

CHRISTMAS

FELT GINGERBREAD MAN
by Beth Edmondson

This hand-sewn felt decoration is quick to make for
last-minute trimmings to the Christmas tree.

You Will Need

Ginger felt

Red ric rac

Orange, red and black
stranded cotton (floss)

Three small buttons

Toy filling

Narrow satin ribbon

2 HOURS

EASY PEASY

1. Use the template to cut two
gingerbread men from the felt. Set
one piece aside for the back and
prepare to decorate the front.

2. Work the facial details using
two strands of embroidery thread:
use black thread to stitch two
large cross stitch eyes, working a
second stitch over the first, and
backstitch a smile; overlap two cross
stitches in red thread for the nose.

3. Sew on three small buttons
down the middle of the gingerbread
man. Cut four pieces of ric rac
each measuring 6cm (2⅜in),
and sew in place at the ankles
and wrists with running stitch.

4. Pin the back and front pieces
together, right sides facing out.
Starting at the shoulder, stitch
using blanket stitch and two strands
of orange embroidery thread.

5. Keep stitching until you reach
the other shoulder, then begin
stuffing. Push the toy filling into the
body, ensuring the hands and feet
are well padded. Cut a length of
ribbon for a hanging loop and stitch
to the inside of the back of the head.

6. Continue blanket stitching
around the head: with about 2cm
(¾in) to stitch, stuff the head
before completing the stitching.

Full-size templates for this project are available at: www.stitchcraftcreate.co.uk

CHRISTMAS

FESTIVE PLACEMATS
by Ali Burdon

This beautiful set of four placemats looks wonderful and is pleasingly simple to make for a festive Christmas table setting.

You Will Need

0.5m (20in) plain red cotton fabric 112cm (44in) wide

0.75m (30in) patterned red fabric 112cm (44in) wide

0.5m (20in) fusible fleece

Red sewing thread

1 DAY

GET STUCK IN

1. Cut eight pieces of plain fabric (A) measuring 33cm x 27cm (13in x 10½in). Cut eight pieces of patterned fabric (B) measuring 14cm x 28cm (5½in x 11in). Cut four pieces of fusible fleece measuring 33cm x 25cm (13in x 10in); fix centrally onto four pieces of fabric A. Pair up pieces of fabric A, right sides together, and stitch the long edges with a 1cm (⅜in) seam allowance. Turn right side out and press.

2. Press seam allowance (1cm/⅜in) on both long edges of fabric B pieces. Mark a line 6cm (2⅜in) parallel to an open edge of the pressed placemat and place one of the fabric B folds against this line, right sides together, with the seam allowance towards the open edge of the mat (fabric B will overhang the mat at the top and bottom edge). Pin and stitch along the line. Repeat on the other side of the mat working with mirror image fabric B piece.

3. Fold the short sides of fabric B in towards the mat and press. Wrap the fabric round to the back of the mat; pin, then slipstitch the sides and long folded edge to the mat to bind the edge. Bind the other edge in the same way. Topstitch each mat, making a line of stitching round the edge of fabric A, about 6mm (¼in) from the edge/seam line.

SNOWFLAKE GIFT BOXES

by Marion Elliot

These little gift boxes make the perfect containers for small, light gifts that can be hung on the tree. Even unfilled they make great tree decorations.

You Will Need

Thick patterned paper

Metallic-gold pearl card size A4 (US letter)

Silk ribbons

30 MINUTES

EASY PEASY

1. Trace and transfer the box template to the back of a sheet of gold card. Cut out.

2. Use a metal ruler and the points of a pair of scissors to score along the fold lines (marked with a dashed line). Fold along the scored lines. Spread glue along the tabs and assemble the box making sure the edges are neatly aligned.

3. Trace and transfer the snowflake template to the back of a sheet of patterned paper and cut out and attach to the front of the box. (For the variation, repeat steps 1 and 2 but cut the box from patterned paper and the snowflake from gold card.)

4. Tie a piece of ribbon around each box. Tie the ribbon into a bow. Trim one end of the ribbon short, leaving the other one long, so you can hang the box from the tree.

Full-size templates for this project are available at: www.stitchcraftcreate.co.uk

CHRISTMAS

CHRISTMAS TREE CARDS
by Debbie Pyne

Use felt, fabric scraps, seed beads and stitching to create a Christmas tree design for these festive greetings cards.

You Will Need

Green patterned fabric

Green felt

Seed beads

Gold or silver thread

White single-fold card size A5

30 MINUTES

GET STUCK IN

1. Use the templates to cut out the Christmas tree shapes from the green patterned fabric and felt. Fold over the edges of the fabric piece as marked on the template and iron in place. Overlap the pieces to form the Christmas tree shape and pin in place.

2. Using a running stitch and gold or silver thread, stitch around the outside edges of the tree pieces to attach them together and to create a decorative border. As you stitch around the shapes, thread a seed bead onto the thread at equally spaced intervals for the baubles.

3. Stick the fabric tree onto the white single-fold card using PVA glue. If making the tiered tree, use a pencil to lightly mark seven dots in a star shape at the top of the tree. Sew a seed bead over each dot, making sure the thread is tied off neatly on the inside of the card.

Full-size templates for this project are available at: www.stitchcraftcreate.co.uk

CHRISTMAS

KNITTED CHRISTMAS PUDS
by Claire Garland

These sweet little treats are made of yarn and sadly can't be eaten! However, they do make very pretty tree decorations – and great present toppers too!

You Will Need

Set 2.5mm (US size 1) double-pointed needles

3mm (US size C/2) crochet hook

1 x 50g ball Rowan Felted Tweed DK brown (A)

1 x 25g ball Patons Fab DK Acrylic Yarn cream (B)

Toy filling

Green felt

Red sewing thread

2 HOURS

GET STUCK IN

1. Knit the Christmas puddings following the pattern below:
Using 2.5mm double-pointed needles and yarn A, cast on 6sts and knit one row as follows: k6, slide sts to the top end/other end of the dpn bring working yarn around back – across sts at the back – and k6 across the front.

Divide sts, slip purl-wise, equally over 3 dpns.
Place stitch marker and begin to knit in the round.
Rnd 1: (inc) Kf&b all sts. 12sts
Rnds 2, 4, 6, 8, 10, 12, 13: K.
Rnd 3: (inc) [K1, kf&b] 6 times. 18sts
Rnd 5: (inc) [K2, kf&b] 6 times. 24sts
Rnd 7: (inc) [K3, kf&b] 6 times. 30sts
Rnd 9: (inc) [K4, kf&b] 6 times. 36sts
Rnd 11: (inc) [K8, kf&b] 4 times. 40sts
Change to yarn B.

Rnd 14: K40.
Rnd 15: (dec) [K8, sl1, kl, psso] four times. 36sts
Rnds 16, 18, 20, 22, 24: K.
Rnd 17: (dec) [K4, sl1, kl, psso] 6 times. 30sts
Rnd 19: (dec) [K3, sl1, kl, psso] 6 times. 24sts
Rnd 21: (dec) [K2, sl1, kl, psso] 6 times. 18sts
Stuff pudding with toy filling.
Rnd 23: (dec) [K1, sl1, kl, psso] 6 times. 12sts
Rnd 25: (dec) Sl1, kl, psso 6 times. 6sts
Cut yarn, thread end through yarn needle, pass needle through rem 6sts, pull up tight to close hole, then secure the end

2. To make the sauce 'drips', make 38 chain using yarn B and crochet hook. Fasten off. Wrap the chain around the pudding securing with yarn or sewing thread as you go around.

3. Cut out holly leaves from green felt and sew in place on top of the pudding with French knot 'berries' worked with red sewing thread.

Full-size templates for this project are available at: www.stitchcraftcreate.co.uk

CHRISTMAS

RIBBON STOCKING
by Carol May

This pretty Christmas tree decoration is made from two ribbons interwoven to create the stocking front.

You Will Need

Fat quarter cotton fabric

Two 1.5m (1¾yd) lengths of contrasting ribbon

Polyester wadding (batting)

2 HOURS

GET STUCK IN

1. Use the template to cut two stockings from the cotton fabric. Set one piece aside for the back and prepare to decorate the front.

2. Taking one of your chosen ribbons, cut and pin strips diagonally across the stocking front. Interweave with strips of contrasting ribbon and pin in place. To securely fix the ribbon in place, machine or hand stitch around the edge of the stocking.

3. Place the two stocking shapes together with right sides facing and stitch around the edge, leaving the top open for turning. Snip carefully into the seam and turn the stocking through to the right side.

4. Stuff the stocking with a small amount of polyester wadding. Turn in the raw edges along the top edge, inserting a hanging loop as shown in the photograph, and slip stitch together.

Full-size templates for this project are available at: www.stitchcraftcreate.co.uk

CHRISTMAS

MINI GINGERBREAD HOUSE
by Fiona Pearce

These tiny gingerbread houses, which are made to sit perfectly on the edge
of a teacup or glass, are ideal place names for the Christmas table.

You Will Need

One batch of
gingerbread dough

White royal icing

Red sugarpaste

Small heart cutter

Disposable piping bag

No. 2 piping nozzle

2 HOURS

GET STUCK IN

1. Use the templates to cut the gingerbread house pieces (front/back, roof and side) from card.

2. Roll out the gingerbread dough to 5mm (³⁄₁₆in). Use the card templates to cut two of each shape from the dough for each house to be made. Using a small knife, score windows into the house sides before baking gingerbread according to the recipe.

3. Allow the gingerbread pieces to cool before assembling and decorating. Fill piping bag fitted with a no. 2 nozzle with stiff peak white royal icing and use to attach the house front, back and sides where the surfaces join.

4. Attach the roof, then pipe a row of dots down the centre of the roof and under the eaves for decoration.

5. Decorate the roof with royal icing patterns. Alternatively, if you are using the gingerbread house as a place card, pipe on a name.

6. Roll out the red sugarpaste to 3mm (¹⁄₈in) thick. Use the small heart cutter to cut out two hearts for each house. Attach the hearts with a small dot of royal icing to the gable ends. Allow the royal icing to dry completely.

Full-size templates for this project are available at: www.stitchcraftcreate.co.uk

CHRISTMAS

PATCHWORK STARS
by Anna Wilson

These patchwork-style star decorations are made from patterned papers, glitter, ribbon and buttons and are perfect to top your Christmas tree.

You Will Need

Patterned papers

Medium-weight card

Polyester filling

Glitter glue

Ribbons

Buttons

1 HOUR

EASY PEASY

1. Print out the rhombus template and add a tab to one of the sides on the bottom triangle. Glue to a piece of card and cut out.

2. Using the card template, cut out 12 rhombuses from your chosen papers for each star. You will be making two patchwork stars for each decoration, one for the back and one for the front. Stick six rhombuses together to make a star using narrow double-sided tape on the tabs. Repeat to make a second star.

3. Place strips of double-sided tape along the edges of the back of one of the patchwork stars. Place a small amount of polyester filling in the middle of the star, then remove the backing from the double-sided tape and put the other patchwork star on top, wrong side facing down, pressing firmly to stick the two stars together.

4. Punch a hole in one of the points and thread a piece of ribbon through for hanging.

5. Embellish the front and back of the patchwork star decoration with buttons and glitter glue.

Full-size templates for this project are available at: www.stitchcraftcreate.co.uk

CHRISTMAS

HANGING BOBBLE HATS
by Claire Garland

Decorate your Christmas tree with a garland of miniature knitted hats
in assorted colours with bobbles knitted in contrast shades.

You Will Need

Set 3.5mm (US size 4)
knitting needles

1 x 50g ball Rowan Baby
Alpaca DK in colours
of your choosing

Green ric rac

Pompom maker set

1 DAY

GET STUCK IN

1. Knit the hats following the
pattern below:

Cast on 36 sts. Divide evenly over 3
needles slipping purlwise, join in the
round.
Rnd 1: [K2, P2] 9 times. Place
marker.
Rnd 2: P.
Rep last 2 rnds 8 times.
Cast off in rib.

2. Take one of the knitted
hat pieces and turn up the ribbed
brim. Then at the cast on edge,
thread up the tail end and work a
running stitch all the way around.
Pull up the stitches to create the
hat shape, and secure the end.

3. Make small pompoms. Sew
a pompom securely in place at the
top of the hat to hide the stitching.

4. Sew on a loop of yarn at
the top of the bobble for hanging.
Thread the completed hats onto a
length of ric rac to make a garland.

5. For an advent calendar,
make 24 hats; embroider each with
a number (1 to 24) worked with
yarn, or use a marker to write the
numbers onto 24 wooden pegs
and attach to a length of ribbon.

CHRISTMAS

PUDDING PLACEMATS
by Denise Mutton

These fun placemats shaped like Christmas puddings
are sure to become a family favourite.

You Will Need

Brown, cream, green
and red felt

Wadding (batting)

Brown stranded cotton (floss)

Fabric adhesive spray

> 1 HOUR
>
> GET STUCK IN 🎁🎁

1. Using a large tea plate as
a template, cut two circles from
brown felt, one circle from wadding
and a half-circle from cream felt.
Cut the bottom edge of the cream
half-circle with a wavy edge.

2. Cut two green felt holly leaves
and three small circles from red
felt for berries. Use brown thread to
sew French knots randomly over the
bottom half of the brown felt circle.

3. Trim the wadding circle by
2.5cm (1in) all round. Layer up
the brown felt circle, the wadding
circle and the embroidered brown
felt circle. Use the fabric adhesive
spray to glue the cream felt in place
at the top of the layered pudding.

4. Blanket stitch around
the edge of the pudding using
brown thread. Sew the holly
leaves and berries to the top.

CUTE CRACKERS
by Ellen Kharade

These crackers made from stiff pastel papers are the prettiest way to gift wrap those small Christmas gifts, such as jewellery. Each takes about an hour to make.

You Will Need

Patterned paper 15cm x 15cm (6in x 6in)

Pink, blue, mint and lavender paper

Cardboard tubes

Felt flowers, small buttons and narrow ribbons

1 HOUR

EASY PEASY

1. Cut one cardboard tube to 7cm (2¾in) and two tubes to 5cm (2in). Apply a strip of narrow double-sided tape to the inside rim of one end of each of the short tubes.

2. Cut a strip of patterned paper measuring 7cm x 16.5cm (2¾in x 6½in). Cut two strips of plain paper measuring 8cm x 16.5cm (3⅛in x 6½in). Using thin masking tape stick the long sides of the plain paper to the long sides of the patterned paper.

3. Cover the patterned paper back with wide double-sided tape strips. Cover one long edge and two short edges with narrow double-sided tape strips. Peel off the backing from the patterned paper; lay the large tube in the centre. Lay the shorter tubes either side leaving a 6mm (¼in) gap in between. Tightly roll the paper around the tubes.

4. To crease the paper into a cracker shape, tie some embroidery thread around the gaps between the

tubes, pull tight and knot several times. Peel off the backing paper from the plain paper and secure around the smaller tubes. Peel off the backing paper from the ends of the tubes and fold in the paper.

5. Decorate the cracker ends with strips of paper cut from co-ordinating paper. Decorate the centre top with felt flowers, with a small button in the centre. Tie long lengths of co-ordinating ribbon into bows around the cracker sections.

CHRISTMAS

COSY WINTER SCARF
by Alison Baker

This lovely self-lined cotton scarf has a snowflake embroidered pocket
at either end to keep your hands warm on long winter walks.

You Will Need

Fabric for scarf:
One piece 148cm x 52cm
(58⅛in x 20¾in)

Fabric for pockets:
Two pieces 27cm x 23cm
(10½in x 9in)

Blue and green stranded
cotton (floss)

2 HOURS

GET STUCK IN

1. Using a fine pencil draw
a snowflake shape on the right
side of each of the pocket
pieces taking care to make
sure the motifs are centred.

2. Embroider the snowflakes
using two strands of embroidery
thread with a decorative stitch
of your choosing, such as
backstitch, for example.

3. Fold the scarf fabric in half
lengthways with right sides together.
Machine stitch with a 1.5cm (⅝in)
seam allowance along the three
open sides, starting at one folded
edge and leaving a 10cm (4in) gap
at the opposite end for turning.

4. Turn the scarf through
to the right side and press.
Sew up the gap by hand.

5. Neaten the edges of the
pocket pieces with machine zigzag
stitch and press over to the wrong
side by 1.5cm (⅝in). Sew along
the top edge using blanket stitch
and two strands of embroidery
thread. Place the pockets at
either end of the scarf aligning the
edges. Tack (baste) the pockets in
place, then machine sew. Remove
the tacking (basting) stitches
from the pockets to finish.

CHRISTMAS

PAPER SNOWFLAKES
by Marion Elliot

These pretty paper decorations are very simple to make for the Christmas tree. The trick to getting really good results is to measure carefully before making each fold.

You Will Need

Double-sided patterned papers

Ribbon for hanging

Ruler

30 MINUTES

EASY PEASY

1. Cut three 1.5cm (⅝in) wide strips of double-sided patterned paper. Cut each strip in half, then fold each of the strips in half.

2. Starting from the middle of a strip make three concertina folds 1cm (⅜in) apart. Fold up the ends of the strips by 1cm (⅜in) to make six branches for each snowflake. Glue the sides of each branch together leaving the ends unglued.

3. Cut a 1.5cm (⅝in) wide strip of paper measuring 7.5cm (3in) long. Glue the ends of the paper strip together to make a circle about 4cm (1½in) in diameter.

4. Glue the snowflake branches around the paper circle, making sure that they are evenly spaced out. To hang the decoration from your tree, you will need to attach a length of ribbon.

CHRISTMAS TREE FAIRY
by Claire Garland

Adorning the top of the Christmas tree with this knitted fairy, with her lovely hand-sewn dress and glittery wings, is sure to become a family tradition.

You Will Need

Set 2.5mm (US size 0) double-pointed needles

1 x 50g ball Patons Fairytale 4 Ply pink

Patterned fabric for dress: Two pieces 8cm x 13cm (3⅛in x 5in)

Sewing thread: white, blue, pale pink, gold, and colour to match patterned fabric

White felt

Silver glitter glue

2 DAYS

FANCY A CHALLENGE

1. Knit the fairy following the pattern below:

Head and body
Cast on 10sts onto one needle then complete the cast on as follows:
Step 1: Hold needle with sts in left hand.
Step 2: Hold 2 empty dpns parallel in right hand.

Step 3: Slip 1st cast on st purlwise onto the dpn closest to you and off the needle in the left hand, then slip the next cast on st onto the dpn furthest away and off the RH needle. Repeat step 3 until all 10 sts are divided onto the 2 parallel dpns, 5sts on the front dpn and 5sts on the back.
Slide sts to the other ends of the

dpns, working yarn at back.
RS facing, cont working in the rnd, beginning by knitting the sts on the back dpn – work sts over 2 dpns, using a 3rd dpn to knit with:
Rnd 1: K10. Place marker.
Rep last rnd 11 times. Stuff the head.
Rnd 13: (dec) K2 tog, k1, sl1, kl, psso, k2 tog, k1, sl1, kl, psso. 6sts (3 sts on each needle)

Rnds 14, 15, 17: K.

Rnd 16: (inc) Kf&b, k1, kf&b, kf&b, k1, kf&b. 10sts

Rnd 18: (inc) Kf&b, k3, kf&b, kf&b, k3, kf&b. 14sts

Rnd 19: K14.

Rep last rnd 14 times.

Stuff the head and body lightly with some spare yarn or scrap of toy stuffing.

Rnd 34: (dec) K3, sl1, k1, psso, k2, k3, sl1, k1, psso, k2. 12sts

Divide for legs

Rnd 35: K3, slip next 3sts off the needle and onto a safety pin, slip next 3sts, from back needle, off the needle and onto another safety pin, knit next 3sts onto the second needle – 3sts on one needle, 3sts on the other.

Rnd 36: *K6.

Rep last rnd until the leg measures approximately 10cm (4in).

Next rnd: (dec) K3 tog twice. 3sts Cut yarn, thread end through 3sts, pull up and secure the end.**

Slip 2 sets of 3sts which are held on the safety pins onto 2 dpns and work the second leg as the first from * to **. If there is a gap between the legs just work a couple of stitches to close it.

Arms (make 2)

Leaving a long tail end (you will use this to sew the arm to the body later), cast on 4sts, *k4, slide sts to the top end/other end of the dpn bring working yarn around back – across sts at the back – and k4 across the front** to create an i-cord. Cont working the i-cord, from * to ** until it measures 6cm (2⅜in).

Next rnd: (dec) K2 tog twice. 2sts Cut yarn, thread end through 2sts, pull up and secure the end. Join the arms to the sides of the body using the tail ends.

2. Work the fairy's facial details. For the mouth, sew a tiny straight line in black sewing thread. To form the eyes, work a few small stitches in blue sewing thread over and over each other symmetrically on either side of the head. Add pale pink stitches to form the cheeks.

3. Now work the fairy's hair using the gold coloured sewing thread. Cut a few 20cm (8in) lengths of thread. Using a few lengths of thread at a time, fold in half to form a loop. Thread the four cut ends through the eye of a needle, then thread the needle through a knitted stitch at the top of the head, but do not pull the thread through fully – instead pass the needle through the loop and pull through until the loop lies flat on top of the head. Work as many strands of hair as you consider necessary.

4. To make the fairy's dress, take the two pieces of patterned fabric and place together with right sides facing. Using a 6mm (¼in) seam allowance, machine or hand stitch along the two long edges leaving a 1.3cm (½in) gap on each side 1.3cm (½in) down from the top edge for the armholes. Turn up a 6mm (¼in) hem at the bottom edge and sew in place. Press a 6mm (¼in) hem at the neck edge, then work a running stitch all the way around the edge; gather up the stitches, just enough so that you can still fit the doll's head inside the neck, then secure the thread. Turn under the raw ends at the armholes and oversew to neaten. Slip the finished dress onto the knitted fairy.

5. Use the template to cut a pair of wings from the felt. Decorate her toes and the wings with glitter glue – this will also stiffen the wings. Once the wings are dry, sew them onto the back of the fairy's dress.

Full-size templates for this project are available at: www.stitchcraftcreate.co.uk

CHRISTMAS

CROSS STITCH PILLOW
by Jayne Schofield

This festive gingerbread man cross stitch design is mounted on a miniature red felt cushion embellished with a pompom braid edging.

You Will Need

White 14-count aida

Green, gold, rust, light pink, lime, blue, lilac and red stranded cotton (floss): DMC colours 912, 676, 402, 963, 3819, 3807, 211 and 666

Two pieces red felt 15.5cm x 15.5cm (6in x 6in)

White and green sewing thread

Green pompom braid

Toy filling

1 DAY

GET STUCK IN

1. Cross stitch the gingerbread man design onto the aida following the chart in the Charts section, using two strands of stranded cotton for the cross stitch and one strand for the backstitch as listed in the chart key. Trim your finished embroidery as shown on the charted design. Lightly press your work on the wrong side.

2. Using white sewing thread and a small running stitch, sew the embroidered design onto one of the red felt squares, positioning it centrally. Place the red felt squares together with the embroidered design facing outwards, and oversew around the edges with tiny stitches leaving a 4cm (1½in) gap for stuffing.

3. Stuff the cushion with toy filling and sew up the gap. Sew the pompom braid around the edges of the cushion using green sewing thread.

CHRISTMAS

SANTA COOKIE LOLLIES
by Ruth Clemens

Christmas is coming and Santa's on his way – enchant everyone with these cute cookie lollies.

You Will Need

Six circular cookies baked on lolly sticks

White sugarpaste

Red and peach gel paste colours

White royal icing

Black icing pen

Circular cookie cutter 8cm (3⅛in) diameter

Disposable piping bag

Small open star piping nozzle

Small embossing rolling pin

1. Colour portions of white sugarpaste red and peach. Roll out the peach sugarpaste to 3mm (⅛in) thick and cut out six circles to cover the cookies, securing in place with a light brush of water.

2. Roll out red sugarpaste 3mm (⅛in) thick and cut out six circles; cut away the bottom two-thirds of each circle with the cutter to create hats. Secure the hats to the cookies. Use the wrong end of the piping nozzle to mark Santa's smile.

3. Roll out white sugarpaste to 2mm (³⁄₃₂in) thick, then go over it with a small embossing rolling pin to imprint a pattern. Cut out 10 circles, then use the cutter to cut away the top one-third from six of the circles to create the beard.

4. Dividing the remaining four circles into thirds, cut away the outside edge to create the moustache pieces. Secure the beard then the moustache onto Santa's face.

5. Make six small peach sugarpaste ball noses and secure each in place. Using a piping bag fitted with the small open star piping nozzle, pipe a royal icing fur trim to the hat. Add Santa's eyes with the black icing pen.

1½ HOURS

GET STUCK IN

SNOWMAN CARD
by Leanne Tough

This simple card design is quick and easy to make for busy crafters during the festive season.

You Will Need

White single-fold card
15.5cm x 15.5cm (6in x 6in)

Patterned paper

White card

30 MINUTES

EASY PEASY

1. Cut a piece of patterned paper to cover just over half of the front of the single-fold card.

2. To make the snowman cut three circles, one 4cm (½in) in diameter, one 2.5cm (1in) in diameter and one 1.5cm (⅝in) in diameter from white card. Glue the circles together, slightly overlapping them.

3. Cut a snowy mound from white card ensuring that the lowest sections measure at least 5.5cm (2¼in).

4. Glue the patterned paper to the top of the single-fold card and use 3D foam adhesive pads to attach the snowy mound to the base of the card so that the mound overlaps the patterned paper.

5. For the snowflakes use a hole punch to punch out lots of small circles from the white card. Glue the snowflakes onto the patterned paper and attach the snowman using 3D foam adhesive pieces. Draw in the details on the snowman with felt-tip pens to finish.

HEXAGONAL BOXES
by Ellen Kharade

These six-sided boxes are perfect for those special gifts at Christmas –
simply fill with treats and embellish with pretty paper flowers or stars.

You Will Need

Patterned papers
30cm x 30cm (12in x 12in)

White card size A4 (US letter)

Mini buttons

Narrow ribbons, ric rac
and flower braid

1 HOUR

EASY PEASY

1. Trace the box base template onto white card and cut out carefully using a craft knife and a metal ruler. Score along the dashed lines, taking care not to cut through the card; fold into shape. Use stick glue to apply adhesive along the box flaps and stick the sides together to construct the box base. Cut a strip of patterned paper measuring 3.5cm x 35cm (1⅜in x 13¾in) and stick it all the way around the sides of the box base.

2. Stick a length of ric rac or flower braid around the sides of the box to decorate, making sure to position it centrally.

3. Trace the box lid template onto white card; cut out and make up as the box base. Cut a hexagon from co-ordinating paper and stick to the top of the box lid. Trace the small hexagon, cut out from plain paper and stick to the centre of the lid box.

4. Use the flower template to cut two flowers from co-ordinating paper. Stick one flower onto the small hexagon. Fold the second flower into shape then stick it on top of the first. Glue a mini button in the middle of the flower.

5. Decorate the rim of the box lid with a 1cm (⅜in) wide strip of patterned paper, and embellish with a narrow ribbon.

Full-size templates for this project are available at: www.stitchcraftcreate.co.uk

CHRISTMAS

KNITTING AND CROCHET

Crochet

Some projects require very simple crochet using a crochet hook. Always start by creating a slip knot and then crochet a chain to the length specified in the pattern.

slip knot   chain

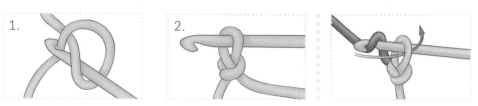

1.   2.

Knitting abbreviations

Abbreviations are used in knitting patterns to shorten commonly used terms so that the instructions are easier to read and a manageable length. The following is a list of the abbreviations you need to make the projects in this book. All knitting patterns in this book use UK terminology. The tinted panel below lists the most common differences between US and UK knitting terms.

beg .... beginning
cm .... centimetre(s)
cont .... continue
dec(s) .... decrease/decreasing
DK .... double knitting
dpn(s) .... double-pointed needles
g .... gram(s)
inc .... increase(s)/increasing
in(s) .... inch(es)
k .... knit
k2tog .... knit 2 stitches together
                (1 stitch decreased)
kf&b .... knit into front and back of
                stitch (1 stitch increased)
LH .... left hand
m1 .... make 1 (1 stitch increased)
MB .... make bobble
mm .... millimetres
oz .... ounces
p .... purl
patt(s) .... pattern(s)
prev .... previous
psso .... pass slipped stitches over
p2tog .... purl 2 stitches together
                (1 stitch decreased)
rem .... remain/remaining

rep(s) .... repeat(s)
RH .... right hand
rnd .... round
RS .... right side
sl .... slip
sl st .... slip stitch
sp(s) .... space(s)
st st .... stocking (stockinette) stitch
                (1 row k, 1 row p)
st(s) .... stitch(es)
tbl .... through back of loop
tog .... together
WS .... wrong side
yon .... yarn over needle
*** .... repeat directions following * as many
                times as indicated or to end of row
( ) .... repeat instructions in round brackets

knitting terms

UK term	US term
stocking stitch	stockinette stitch
cast off	bind off
tension	gauge

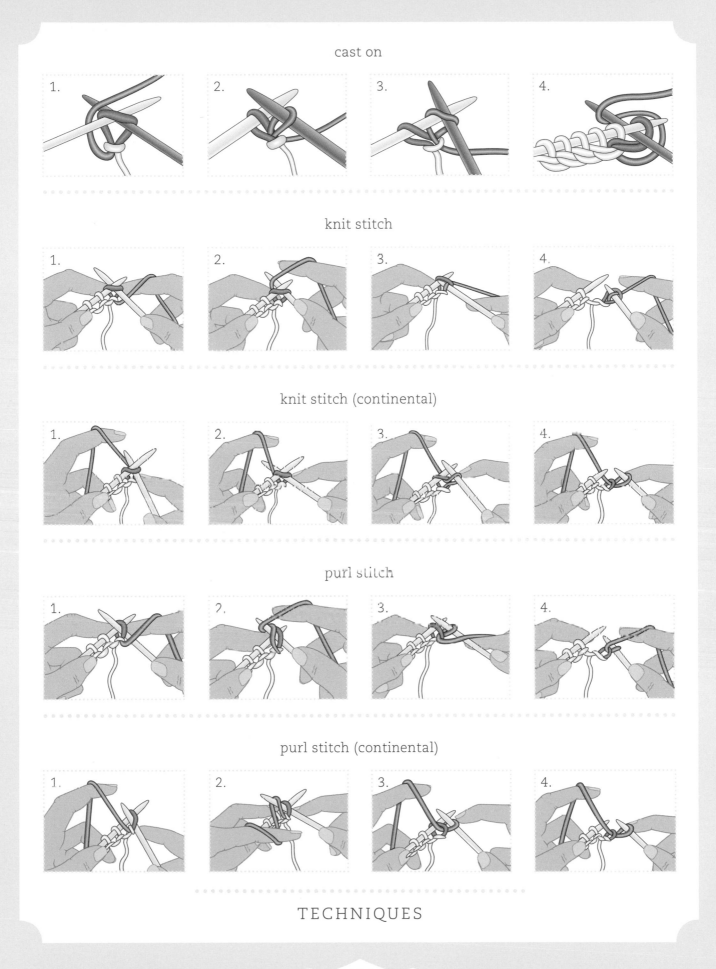

cast on

knit stitch

knit stitch (continental)

purl stitch

purl stitch (continental)

TECHNIQUES

Knitting in the round

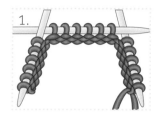

Grafting

Working from right to left, insert the tapestry needle from the back of the work through the first stitch on each edge and pull the yarn through. Continue in this way, forming a new row of stitches.

I-cord

1. Cast on a small number of stitches on a circular or double-pointed needle. Push the stitches to the other end of the needle and turn the needle, so the first stitch you'll knit is the first one you cast on.

2. Knit the stitches, making sure you pull the yarn tight for the first stitch. Move the stitches to the other end of the needle. Repeat this process until the i-cord is the desired length.

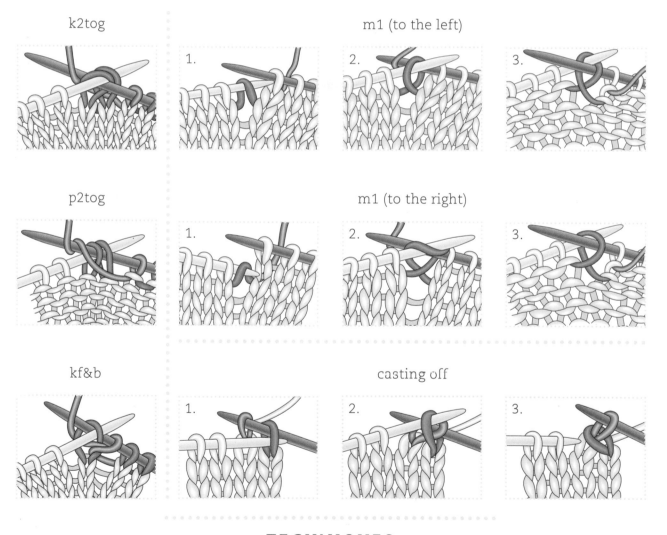

k2tog

m1 (to the left)
1. 2. 3.

p2tog

m1 (to the right)
1. 2. 3.

kf&b

casting off
1. 2. 3.

SEWING

Basic stitches

When sewing by hand choose a needle that matches the thickness of the thread you are using, so the thread passes easily through the fabric. All stitches can be started with a knot on the back of the work and finished off neatly at the back, usually with backstitch.

backstitch

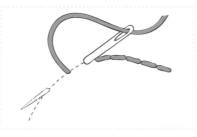

running stitch

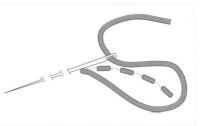

cross stitch

blanket stitch

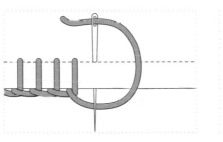

French knot

whip stitch (oversew)

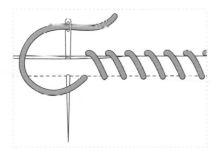

hem stitch

ladder stitch

slip stitch

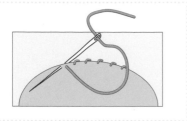

topstitch

BEADING

Half hitch knot

Take the needle behind a thread between beads and pull through leaving a loop. Pass the needle back through the loop and pull up to make the half-hitch. Work a second half hitch a few beads along for extra security, applying a drop of jewellery glue before trimming the tail.

Overhand knot

Cross the tail over the main thread to make a small loop, then pass the tail under the thread and back through the loop. Pull on each end of the thread to tighten the knot. You can manoeuvre the knot into position with a tapestry needle.

CHARTS

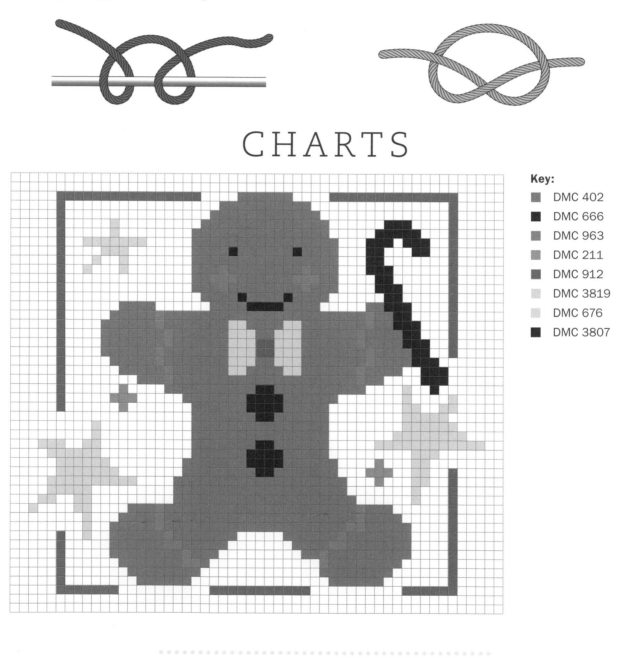

Key:
- DMC 402
- DMC 666
- DMC 963
- DMC 211
- DMC 912
- DMC 3819
- DMC 676
- DMC 3807

TECHNIQUES

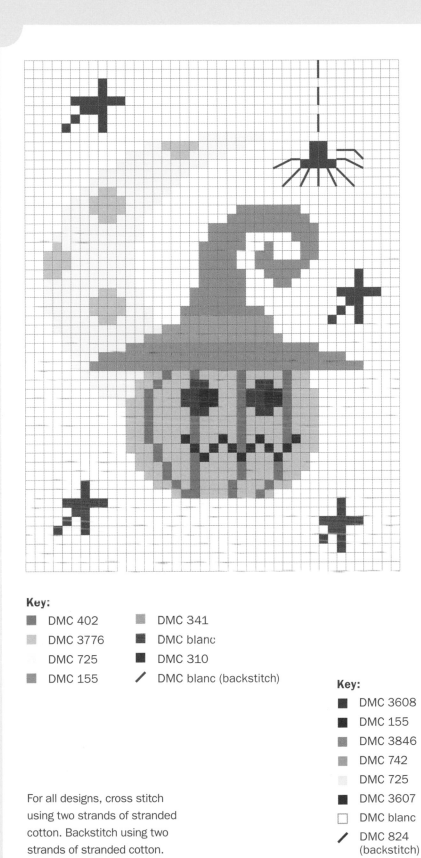

Key:

- ■ DMC 402
- ■ DMC 3776
- DMC 725
- ■ DMC 155
- ■ DMC 341
- ■ DMC blanc
- ■ DMC 310
- ╱ DMC blanc (backstitch)

For all designs, cross stitch using two strands of stranded cotton. Backstitch using two strands of stranded cotton.

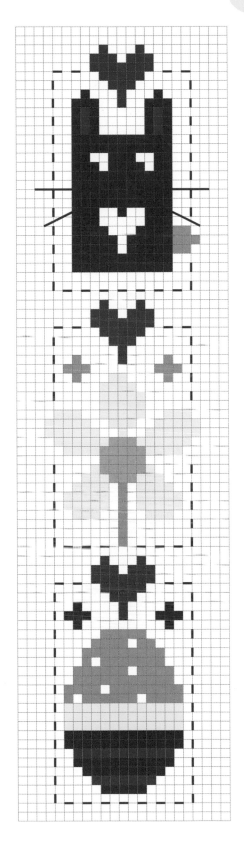

Key:

- ■ DMC 3608
- ■ DMC 155
- ■ DMC 3846
- ■ DMC 742
- DMC 725
- ■ DMC 3607
- □ DMC blanc
- ╱ DMC 824 (backstitch)

TECHNIQUES

SUPPLIERS

Materials to make the projects in this book can be found at:
www.stitchcraftcreate.co.uk

ACKNOWLEDGMENTS

The publishers would like to thank all of the contributors
whose designs have been featured in this book:

Chloe Adcock	Beth Edmondson	Jane Millard
Charlotte Addison	Marion Elliot	Denise Mutton
Jenny Arnott	Mary Fogg	Fiona Pearce
Alison Baker	Claire Garland	Debbie Pyne
James Brooks	Jennifer Grace	Emily Rodger
Ali Burdon	Sarah Joyce	Prudence Rogers
Susan Burley	Kate Kerly	Jayne Schofield
Louise Butt	Ellen Kharade	Leanne Tough
Rosina Cassam	Zoe Larkins	Sue Trevor
Ruth Clemens	Danielle Lowy	Anna Wilson
Linda Clements	Carol May	Dorothy Wood

SUPPLIERS / ACKNOWLEDGMENTS

INDEX

A DAVID & CHARLES BOOK
© F&W Media International, Ltd 2013

David & Charles is an imprint of F&W Media International, Ltd
Brunel House, Forde Close, Newton Abbot, TQ12 4PU, UK

F&W Media International, Ltd is a subsidiary of F+W Media, Inc
10151 Carver Road, Suite #200, Blue Ash, OH 45242, USA

Text and Designs © F&W Media International, Ltd 2013
Layout and Photography © F&W Media International, Ltd 2013

First published in the UK and USA in 2013

A catalogue record for this book is available from the British Library.

ISBN-13: 978-1-4463-0315-3 paperback
ISBN-10: 1-4463-0315-2 paperback

ISBN-13: 978-1-4463-0314-6 hardback
ISBN-10: 1-4463-0314-4 hardback

Printed in China by RR Donnelley for
F&W Media International, Ltd
Brunel House, Forde Close, Newton Abbot, TQ12 4PU, UK

10 9 8 7 6 5 4 3 2 1

Editor: Jeni Hennah
Project Editor: Cheryl Brown
Senior Designer: Victoria Marks
Photographers: Sian Irvine and Jack Gorman
Senior Production Controller: Kelly Smith

F+W Media publishes high quality books on a wide range of subjects.
For more great book ideas visit: **www.stitchcraftcreate.co.uk**

LOVED THIS BOOK?

For more inspiration, ideas and free downloadable projects visit

www.stitchcraftcreate.co.uk

101 WAYS TO STITCH CRAFT CREATE

Various

ISBN-13: 978-1-4463-0282-8 (UK)

ISBN-13: 978-1-4463-0187-6 (US)

Try your hand at a range of quick and fun crafts. This collection of 101 projects includes sewing, stitching, embroidery, quilting, appliqué, knitting, crochet, papercraft, beading and cake decorating so you can unleash the crafter within you!

STITCH NEW YORK

Lauren O'Farrell

ISBN 13: 978-1-4463-0188-3

Want to knit a neurotic Woolly Woody Allen? Or hail a Small Yellow Taxi that really rolls? From proud and purly Little Lady Liberty, to the Squishy Empire State, to the star-struck Broadway Beanie, Stitch New York is a melting pot of Big Apple knitting patterns.

MAKE ME I'M YOURS... JUST FOR FUN

Various

ISBN-13: 978-1-4463-0069-5

Create 20 unique gifts and accessories, from jewellery and bags to socks and photo frames! Try your hand at a wide range of crafts, including sewing, knitting, crochet, papercraft, needle felting and soap making.

HAPPY STITCH

Jodie Rackley

ISBN-13: 978-1-4403-1857-3

Charming felt and fabric projects that take minutes to make! With a few simple stitches and some basic materials, you'll be crafting in no time at all. From plush animals to electronics cozies and curtains to pillows, you'll love filling your home with bright and colourful crafty creations!